STORIES OF HOPE

Written by Children

Refugee and Oppressed

1

Edited by Dogan Yucel

AST PUBLISHING

STORIES OF HOPE - 1

Written by Children
Refugee and Oppressed

Copyright © AST Publishing, 2022

All publication rights of this work belong to Advocates of Silenced Turkey. All rights reserved. No part of this book may be reproduced or transmitted in any form or by any means, electronic or mechanical, including photocopying, recording or by any information storage and retrieval system without permission in writing from the Advocates of Silenced Turkey.

www.silencedturkey.org

Published: June 2022
ISBN: 9798833606544

Stories of Hope

CONTENTS

About the Hizmet Movement	5
Editor's Note	6
Foreword	9
Dreams Mean Hope	11
We Carried Each Other Through	14
I Want to Tell You That I'm Not Devastated	21
Memories That Took Me Years To Forget	25
Despite Impossibilities	28
My Head Is High and It will Always Remain So	30
Hard Days	34
Near but Far	39
Stars Too Far Away From Each Other	51
Gift Chest	55
I Wish I Didn't Know	57
Close Friend	63
Childhood	67
As We Forget Grief	72
Against Persecution	74
Silent Scream	78
Longing for Family	82
Effort	88
Pistachio Family	91
I Will Be Fair When I Grow Up	95
Ege's Fortunes from Surah Vakia	98

North Stars	102
Love of Father	107
Dad's Shoes	111
The Life Is Beautiful	114
Don't Send Me Anywhere Else Again	118
Feelings	122
We Keep Dreaming	126
Time and Us	130
Bitter And Sweet Moments	136
Those Who Deserve Paradise	138
Tears of Joy	142
Pray for Good Days	145
Past and Future	149
Bravery	153
Normal Course of Events	155
Fathers and Their Jobs	158
Happy Ending	159
Understanding People	164
Unknowns	169
The Last Chocolate	172
Despair	176

Stories of Hope

ABOUT THE HIZMET MOVEMENT

Hizmet is a transnational civil society initiative that advocates for the ideals of human rights, equal opportunity, democracy, non-violence, and the emphatic acceptance of religious and cultural diversity. This widespread movement began in Turkey as a grassroots community in the 1970s in the context of social challenges being faced at the time: violent conflicts among ideologically and politically driven youth, desperate economic conditions, and decades of a state-imposed ideology of discrimination that mandated a particular lifestyle.

Over the years, Hizmet has transformed from a grassroots community in Turkey to a much wider global effort with participants from all walks of life. Their work is centered upon promoting philanthropy and community service, investing in education to cultivate virtuous individuals, organizing intercultural and interfaith dialogue events to promote a more peaceful coexistence.

Hizmet participants are inspired by the ideas and example of Fethullah Gulen, a Muslim scholar who has expressed the belief that serving fellow humans is as serving God.

For more information: www.afsv.org

EDITOR'S NOTE

Advocates of Silenced Turkey (AST) is a non-governmental organization that runs its activities on a voluntary basis since 2018. The aim of AST is to bring before international public opinion the human rights violations including torture and the unlawful court trials and proceedings, which have been encountered in Turkey especially the last ten years. After 2016, more than 160,000 innocent people lost their jobs in both public and private sectors, with accusations and unjust convictions of being connected with the coup attempt. The state of emergency, which was announced on July 20, 2016, gave the government unchecked powers - in the disguise of combatting terrorism - to persecute thousands of people with no accountability and to undermine the fundamental principles of a democratic society and the most basic principles of universal human rights and values such as freedom of expression and freedom of the press. Today, tens of thousands of highly qualified professionals such as judges, prosecutors, doctors, teachers, journalists, academics, and military officers have been detained and imprisoned in Turkey due to bogus terrorism charges. Around 5,000 of them are women, along with nearly 345 children who stay with their mothers in prisons. Hundreds of thousands of people have little or no hope of surviving the grueling atmosphere in Turkey, and as they are banned from leaving the country, they have no other choice but to flee at the risk of losing their lives by crossing the borders via dangerous routes. Some of them have not survived this difficult journey.

As the Advocates of Silenced Turkey, we engage in a number of activities in order not to keep silent about the injustices that have been taking place in Turkey where the rule of law has been suspended for a long time.

APH (Archiving the Persecution of Hizmet) project of recording and archiving the testimonies of victims, aims to shed light on the injustices suffered by thousands of people in Turkey. Our volunteers have conducted hundreds of interviews and thanks to their efforts, the victimizations, and hardships that the victims experienced are now being recorded in both spoken and written formats. The main purpose of this project is to ensure that these tragic stories are not allowed to fade into oblivion but are rather recorded accurately and impartially to leave firsthand sources for future generations. We also aim to bring this persecution to the attention of academics, media organizations, human rights associations, prominent community leaders, and government representatives at the international level.

"STORIES OF HOPE: Written by Children Refugee and Oppressed" is the product of a long-term endeavor. Each of our works is a compilation of real-life stories encountered by victims whose true names and event details have not been revealed for the safety of their families in Turkey. We would like to thank everyone who made tireless and valuable contributions to this work. We wish that Turkey will soon transform into a democratic society in which fundamental values like universal human rights and the rule of law are duly observed.

Stories of Hope

FOREWORD

The Stories of Hope: Written by Children Refugee and Oppressed is a compiled selection of the stories submitted for the "Hope Stories from Refugee Children" contest, organized by Advocates of Silenced Turkey (AST) in 2022. In this book, you will read the words of children between ages 10 and 18, who were exposed to severe injustices in Turkey and were consequently forced to leave their country, as they narrate various forms of ordeal they suffered. You will see how they look at life, how they interpret the heavy experiences they had to go through and how they deal with them, with the guidance of their modest and unsophisticated illustrations.

From simple strifes to world-shattering upheavals, children bear the brunt of all grievous events. Let's save children from getting lost and crushed. Let's hold onto our future and the future of the world together and give them the opportunity to hold on to life and the future. Let's explain to them that *the good* and *goodness* will always exist and must exist, despite the evils surrounding time and space. We hope the world embraces children, who are the best examples of unending hope, with love.

We believe that this book is a new and strong supplement to our efforts to interpret the psychological, social and economic difficulties experienced by those whose rights and freedoms have been violated. It demonstrates the impact the heavy tribulations had on children from their plain and limpid point of view, without resorting to the intricate rhetorical arts.

The book aims to offer an insight into the grievances and into how traumatic impacts these storms have had on tiny hearts. We cannot claim that we did it flawlessly; on the contrary, despite all our attention, we will have mistakes and shortcomings. In this regard, we thank you, our esteemed and careful readers, for your understanding in advance.

We extend our most sincere gratitudes to everyone who contributed to this work, especially our children who opened their world and hearts to us and emblazoned our hearts with the glimmers of the inspirations of hope. And we surely owe a debt of gratitude to all our volunteers for their support, especially in the organization of the competition, the publication of the works and the awarding of our children. We will never cease to be a voice for the silent cries of helpless and powerless children in the face of injustice in Turkey and all over the world, thanks to the efforts of people devoted to justice and love.

Stories of Hope

DREAMS MEAN HOPE

Written by: Beyza, 17

It's okay if you've already fallen! I fell too… All you have to do is see the helping hand extended towards you and make another effort. Then everything will be better…

Hi! I am Beyza. I was 13 when I learned that my father was expelled from his job. This news turned my life upside down in the blink of an eye and I was trying to adapt to all this change. It was as if the window through which I looked at life suddenly went black. I couldn't even understand what was going on. All these things that were happening around me made me feel so alone and as if I was in a dark void. I recovered thanks to my mother. She never left me alone. Since my father was no longer with us, she had to work and take care of me at the same time.

Thanks to my mother, I was able to pull myself together only after a year and now I am recovering rapidly. No matter what difficulties life throws at me, I will not let myself ride for a fall. This time I don't want someone to take me by the hand. Because I've recently gotten wise to the fact that we are not alone in the world; that there are millions of companions in similar conditions like us. So, instead of being a burden to people, I will now extend my hand to others in any way I can.

Life strikes everyone from different angles: it's not to bring us down but to strengthen our character, preparing us to stand against the events that might threaten us in the future. My condition is better now because I have a lot of people with me. I now have the twinkles of millions of stars in the sky of my little world, illuminating my way, guiding me through. In the light of my experiences , I can also articulate the way we children cope with such situations. First it depends on our spiritual strength and second on the attitude of the people around us. Even though my spiritual strength was low, when I closed my eyes out of fear and pretended that everything was just a dream, I was not desperate. Thanks to my mother for this. She was always by my side and brought me here on her back despite all the other burdens she had to shoulder.

Now, I am trying to adapt to this new place. Thanks to my mom for bringing me here. It is very encouraging to know that you have the firmness of a mountain behind you...

I am now seventeen years old and I will take a college entrance exam next year. This time I will not lose myself. I will study hard and score enough to enroll in the department I want. I am grateful to everything and everyone who has helped me get through this difficult time. What keeps a person alive in these times, in this evil-filled world is just a tiny glimmer of light. A butterfly sometimes, or sometimes a news story that proves that humanity is not dead... Although these seem very small and ordinary, sometimes they can cause a sort of butterfly effect, helping us children cling to life.

My advice to people in dire straits would be to try not to retire into your shells and mind your health. Because, in my case, I gained a lot of weight and became chubby in a very short time. Then I injured my foot while running. If I could go back in time, I would try to find someone to take me out and help me make friends in that year of weight gain. But I'm fine now. I lost my excess weight and regained my health by eating healthy and exercising. Here, I would like to warn millions of children like me that letting go is never the solution and we must act before it's too late. Our health is in our hands, and if it's gone, it's incredibly hard to get it back.

It's okay if you've already fallen! I fell too... All you have to do is see the helping hand extended towards you and make another effort. Then everything will be better... I'm telling you this as someone who has lived through this tribulation before. Surely you have a dream... If you have a dream, you also have hope... Dreaming is not that hard, or it doesn't have to be difficult. Even petting a cat can be a dream. Dream means hope for me. I think you can also find your own hope with only a little bit of effort.

In these difficult times, the greatest need for us children is to believe in ourselves and to have a loving parent. Hard times become easier and full of hope thanks to them. Just the fact that they are standing by us gives us an endless source of energy. Greetings to my mother who stayed by my side when I was in this state and watched over me, to all the colors of life and to the stars that illuminate my path… I cannot repay you. You mean so much to me. I would love to be able to pay what I owe you some day... I think this will be my next dream after the exam I will take next year.

WE CARRIED EACH OTHER THROUGH

Written by: Feyza, 12

At that moment, I felt my eyes welling up, but I shouldn't have cried...

Hi! I'm Feyza. I am twelve years old. Our lives changed overnight. On the night of the coup, we went to a town to visit my father's cousin. The TV was not installed as they had just moved in. We didn't know anything. We were spending time with our relatives and my family was informed of the events by a phone call. I was only seven years old so I couldn't understand anything that they talked about. My mother and father were both fired from their jobs in the same week. Before long, my aunt and cousins came to us and we started living together. My aunt's husband was in prison. We were passing through difficult times, but we were all supporting each other.

One day the bell rang at 07:00 in the morning. I was in the 2nd grade of primary school. I was wearing my dress for a special program at school. The doorbell rang. Honestly, I was really scared. Who could it be in such an early hour of the morning? My mother opened the door. When I saw three male and one female police officers standing in front of the door, I started to get more scared. My mother woke my father up. Then the police began to search the house.

The policewoman asked me to show my tablet and my games. I think she also understood that I was scared. She came over to give me a lift and said, "Don't worry, we won't snatch anything away. We're just going to search your house and go." I believed her. Actually I wasn't aware at that time that they were just about to take away a big piece of my heart… It was time for school. My mother asked the police "to keep my father a little longer since she needs to take me to school." However, I only learned this much later.

I went to school that day. I came back from school but my father was not there. In the evening, my father was still not there. The next day, he was not again. That's when I realized that my father wasn't coming back home.

About a month later, I went to the non-contact visitation to see my father's face for the first time. We didn't inform my father about my coming on the phone call, so he was naturally thinking that the only visitors were my grandmother and mother. After passing through searches in two separate locations, we finally reached the room where we would see my father. When I met my father's eyes, I felt very bad. Because when my father saw me, he could not control his tears. It was the first time in my life that I saw my father so fragile and so fatigued. My father was trying to restrain himself, but as I said, he couldn't stop the tears.

At that moment, I felt my eyes welling up with tears, but I shouldn't have cried, because if I cried, my father would feel even worse. I immediately wiped my tearful eyes with my hands and put my hand on the partition glass. My father did the same. I wanted to hold my father's hand. I wanted to hug him, but the glass that separated us wouldn't allow any of that. I looked into my father's tearful eyes; it was so hard not to cry out loud at that moment. But I had to do it for my father. I pulled myself together and put the phone to my ear and called my father: "Daddy." After waiting for a few seconds and trying to collect himself, my father answered "My lamb" and his eyes filled with tears again. "Don't cry," I said in a tone pretending to stay strong. Then I talked to my father. My mom and grandma talked to him, too. Then it was time for us to part.

It was as if my father was my breath and they were taking my breath away from me. It was like I was suffocating. Then we went outside and my mom and grandma kept crying the whole way home. Seeing them so vulnerable was killing me even more. When we got home it was finally my time to cry; now alone, I could freely unburden my heart.

During the time when we went to non-contact visits, I was doing my best to hold back, and then when I got home, I was bursting into tears. My mother was crying a lot. I sat next to her every time, I hugged her and said, "Don't worry mommy, my dad is not underground. He is still alive on the earth and one day, I hope he will come back home again." Every time my mother heard these words, she was getting a little stronger and was becoming more grateful to Allah. That's how I was consoling myself: My father was above ground, not below, and as long as he's breathing, we should be thankful.

During the time my father was in jail, many sisters and brothers, whose names we do not know, supported us financially and morally. The days we went to the prison visits coincided with the schooldays. We explained this situation to my teacher. He was very touched and said he would help us. I was going to the non-contact visits and then going to school. I was collecting the notes of the courses I couldn't attend from my friends.

Then one day, my mom told me it would be a contact visitation and I could hug and touch my dad. I was in seventh heaven.

The day of the free visit finally arrived. We got up early in the morning and went to the prison. We went through the same search locations again and a hall welcomed us. Some uncles were coming out of a door one after another, hugging their wives and children. We eagerly awaited my father. Then my father came out that door. I felt so different. My father was standing right in front of me and I could hug him. There was no glass separating us. I got up and started running towards my father. I jumped into my father's lap. My father hugged me tightly. I had so much missed hugging him, his scent... My father and I could separate only after a long hug. He hugged my mother, my grandmother, my aunt, my grandfather, and then me again. He put a tender kiss on each of my cheeks.

We sat at a table. I looked around, everyone was so happy, they were hugging each other. We talked to my father. Then a bell rang to alert people that it was time to leave. This bell sound became one of the sounds I hated the most in my life. Outside, my mother and grandmother naturally started to cry again. Surprisingly, this time I couldn't control my tears. Just before my father left back to his ward, he made me a rose from the napkin on the table. I wiped my tears with my hands and received the rose from my father. It was so beautiful and when we got home, I put it in the best place on my desk.

Weeks passed as we were going back and forth for visits and of course there were days when I couldn't attend my classes. I was fabricating excuses to hide my situation from my friends. It hurt me to lie to my friends, but that's how I had to do it. Anyway, as I said, months flew by yet we had never lost our hope. My biggest advantage was my family. We were always by each other's side. We were always ready to give each other a morale boost. We carried one another through.

It has been 9.5 months since my father was put in prison, but believe me, it felt like years. At the end of that 9.5-month period, there was a court hearing for my father. Almost the entire family was in front of the prison. Since nobody knew what decision the court would give, my family did not want to take me and my cousin with them. My aunt also had some health problems and she also couldn't go. So my aunt, cousin and I stayed at home and prayed. Then, when I heard about my father's release decision, I was extremely happy. The withered flowers in me bloomed again. My mother was going to come back to pick us up and take us to prison while my father was preparing to get out. We were so happy that my cousin, my aunt and I cried and hugged each other.

My mom took me and my cousin and my aunt stayed at home to cook until we arrived. There were a total of 4 or 5 cars, including us and some friends of my father. Everyone was there. We were waiting in front of the prison. Then the doors opened. I saw my father outside for the first time in 9.5 months. Even though the officer there told us not to cross the line, my cousin and I could not help ourselves and ran and hugged my father.

My father drove the car on the way home. When my father came home, he also hugged my aunt. It was one of the best moments of my life. Then we left my aunt's house late at night and came to our own house. In the evening I saw my father with a notebook in his hand. He was writing something. When my father finished his writing, I took the notebook and began to read. Before the court hearing, my father had written "Am I at home?" and left the remaining blank. Now he wrote to fill this blank section, writing "Yes, I'm home at 23:00!" I was very emotional. In subsequent trials, the court sentenced him to six years and three months. His case is in the Supreme Court now and we are waiting for the decision. In this process, I comprehended the significance of my family; I grasped that there is always hope no matter what; and I understood the value of happiness.

I WANT TO TELL YOU THAT I'M NOT DEVASTATED

Written by: Sena, 13

I wrote this essay to proclaim that we are still here, that we are not devastated.

Hi! I'm Sena. It's been exactly a year and a half since I was separated from my father, I mean since my father was put in jail. When my father left, we moved in with my mother's family. I realized that when my father was with me, that is, before he left, how insignificant all my troubles were.

As the saying goes, you should always have hope in

life! So let's talk a little bit about hope. A few days ago, I learned one of my father's wardmates was released and I was very happy. He stopped by to see us a few weeks after he was released. We talked about my father. It was nice to know that my father was well off there. He even told his friends there about an event that he did not talk about with us. I want to recount this to you as well.

One day my mother, father and mother's father were sitting at a floor table for dinner, my father said to my mother: "I will go visit my mother." When my mother responded saying, "I am not coming," my father said, "If you don't wish to come along with me, then don't come. I'll go alone." Then my grandfather chipped in, "Son, do you know about **Sürmene** blades?" My father said, "No, I don't." My grandfather said, "They are sharp on both sides. If you stab a man with it, if he doesn't die because of the blade, he will die of blood loss." And then my father said, "No, dad, I was indeed joking." And didn't life stab us like a Sürmene knife? Yet our family is from the Black Sea region; so this time the blade hit a stone wall. And, as they say, when Black Sea folk run out of hope, then their tenacity kicks in. We have never lost hope and never will.

I think this hope and stubbornness thing applies not only to Black Sea people, but to all humanity. I know that there are those who have experienced what we went through, or even worse. But as I said, hope and stubbornness are intrinsic to all humanity. People who were in bed of roses in the past are also going through this ordeal and becoming stronger. I'm sure this following poem by Darvish Yunus may describe to some extent all the people who experience it, if it cannot fully represent them:

"Ye, owner of commodities, man of property.

So where lies its first owner now?

Commodity is a lie, so is property.

You too fool about them for a while."

So, my friends, what I am trying to say is that if you fall and get hurt, rise on your feet and this time run even faster.

I've been meeting new people lately. All of them are in the same situation as mine. They are indeed closer to me than our relatives, seeing that we really have the same wounds and share the same feelings. Think about it, there are many families that experience this, and we only know a few.

My other hope is that my father can be released as well. After all, the future is an unrevealed secret, but it's up to you to live in the present, to live this very moment as well as possible. And perhaps you can choose any day of any season, whether it's summer or winter, and add an eighth to seven days and say, "this is the day my father came." There are so many emotions in life that beggar description. I am sure that when I see my father and hug him, when I hear his voice, I will feel all the emotions with or without a name. May Allah bring together many families who are waiting to be reunited! The morning before my father left, my eldest sister had an argument with him. When we got home from school, we learned that my father was taken away. "I wish my father would beat me again. The pain I feel started to subside," my sister said. No wonder why people say that a rose blossoms where your father hits.

So, put it this way: it is imperative that we get along well with the people around us, with our family, as best as we can while we still have time. It makes me happier to assess all these incidents as a test Allah has set to encourage his servants to win the bliss in the Hereafter. Because my father is a very kind hearted person. It's great when people help each other.

I wrote this essay to proclaim that we are still here, that we are not devastated. I hope we all live a happy life and unite as soon as possible with those who we wait yearningly for.

Stories of Hope

MEMORIES THAT TOOK ME YEARS TO FORGET

Written by: Aybuke

Mentally, I had an anger that I wasn't able to control or resist. I had grown numb to emotions.

There was a TV show my mom and I used to watch and we had waited weeks for the new season. As we were waiting for the new episode to air, we had another surprise: my mother was arrested. I had just started the eighth grade. That is to say, it was the year of taking the high-school exam. My mother was arrested in the first week of school and released after three days.

Let me rewind the story back a bit earlier, that is, to July 15, 2016. We learned about the coup from my aunt, who called us that evening on the phone. Ironically, my mother and father were suspended within a month on charges of aiding the coup they only learned about from others. I believed at that time that they still had a chance to resume their jobs. However, they were later expelled. Then I felt gratitude that they were still with me. But, as I mentioned above, this time my mother was arrested. And I don't know if you'd believe it, but I was thinking that at least my father was still with us. I guess they must have found my optimism too much, because my father was arrested a week before the high school exam. I stayed alone with my brother for about two months, but I was relieved to some extent. Because I had nothing to lose.

Let me touch on different aspects of the process. Financially, we lost our security. Academically speaking, because we were going to Bursa Yenişehir prison for my mother one day and to Balıkesir to visit my father the next day, I had only three school days left in my week. And considering the people's gazes at school, even the roads of Balıkesir started to seem more pleasant. Mentally, I had an anger that I wasn't able to control or resist. I had grown numb to emotions. For example, when my mother got out of prison, I couldn't even hug her. But at the same time, I was like a powder keg, ready to fight with anyone at any moment. I couldn't sleep at night and as this situation started to get more and more annoying, I started using sleeping pills. Frankly, I don't want to go into too much detail. I don't want to revive memories that have already taken me years to forget.

Meanwhile, my mother had her trial at court. Since my father was also in prison, she was released under house arrest as the court considered that there should be someone to look after the children. We were very happy as we didn't expect it at all. My mother was under house arrest for two months but then they removed it, too. So she was able to see my father for the first time in nine months.

We had a car accident on one of our visits to my father's prison. Since we sort of touched that frontier between life and death, even after four years, my mom still has the trauma of an accident every time she gets in the car. (If I talk about everything in detail, I don't think this will end.) Anyway, at the end of eleven months, my father was also released and years later, we started to live as a family again. In this process, I had to send off my best friend abroad. I prepared for the university exam and entered the top 2,000 in Turkey in terms of equally weighted score. I would like to do it better and actually I could have done it better in my opinion, but it happened to be like this.

As for today, my mother was sentenced to 6 years and 10 months and my father was sentenced to 6 years and 3 months, and we are waiting. Mine is an ordinary story like everyone else's. It took two pages to write, but it has already been five years and its effects still linger. It was truly a different experience for me. I really hope it was all worth it. I'm not talking about my own experiences because I've heard of much more unpleasant events.

DESPITE IMPOSSIBILITIES

Written by: Aysel

These atrocities, this persecution will come and go, as long as we never give up the struggle for life.

First of all, it is impossible for me to fully express in writing the process that I went through.

It was so early in a summer morning, the calendar was showing August 4th, there was a knock on the door. Who could be knocking on our door at this hour? My father woke up and went to open the door. He shouted from the door. No matter how much time has passed, that shout is still in my ears: "THE POLICE HAVE COME." We got up from the beds, the whole family. The fear of not knowing what would happen was in the eyes of all of us. How does such a feeling so obviously exist in the eyes? As a result of their searches, nothing was found in the house, but that did not prevent them from detaining my father and taking him away.

Before he left, I made my father have his last breakfast. Fortunately I did so. How could I have known that I would be separate from my father for five years? And my days are still passing without him. He is gone and he is gone for good... At first, we were speculating that he would be back home in a month or, if not, another month at the latest. Now this optimism gave way to despair. We've become numb too.

The trials I attended made me so angry that I learned once again how not to treat people. This process has taught me a lot. Sometimes I think I fortunately have gone through all this. Of course we had a hard time. We can say that it was a process in which my mother was especially worn out. But somehow we got through it. After all, we are human beings; We get used to everything. The idea that everything has a solution except death shows that there is always hope. I believe we were able to get through this process without compromising our own humanity.

I cannot say, however, that my life continued in its usual course aside from all these troubles. The health problems I suffered from during this period affected me deeply. Appointments that we wait grudgingly for at five in the morning, our visits to doctors in other cities, the inability of doctors to diagnose my disease among all the troubles, and more… "You have cancer" or "you have tuberculosis", which the doctors coldly told my mother and I… They indeed drew us to life even more and the bliss of having a life made us stronger. These atrocities, this persecution will come and go, as long as we never give up the struggle for life. If we live a life with zero hassle then, I believe, it would be a little difficult to win paradise. That's why we're still here trying to win paradise. We do our best not to stray from the path of Allah...

MY HEAD IS HIGH AND IT WILL ALWAYS REMAIN SO

Written by: Edanur, 15

For how long will I not hear my father's voice? What will happen to our family now? Were these supposed to be the questions running through the mind of a 15-year-old child!

I'm Edanur, one of the hundreds of children whose life changed, turned upside down. I was bereft of a father at a time when a child needs fatherly affection and guidance the most. Despite being relatively older than many other children exposed to similar ordeals, it was one of the biggest blows I've sustained in my short life.

I still remember the last words my father said when he was being taken away that morning. "Don't cry, my daughter! Would it be better if I were really guilty?" Then I struggled to walk from home to school, sobbing, forcing myself to enter the exam that day. I had dozens of thoughts in my head at that age; Where did my father go? When will he return? For how long will I not hear my father's voice? What will happen to our family now? Were these supposed to be the questions running through the mind of a 15-year-old child?

I was aware of the struggles of my mother during the next 2 years; I won't forget them even if I die. She did the best a mother could do to support and shelter her children, we three siblings... My brother, my younger brother and I. My brother had it harder through this period than any of us. I don't know but maybe it would be appropriate to say that he felt all alone, like an orphan. How much could a mother alone suffice for a big young boy all by herself? I wonder if my brother's wounds have yet healed? Has he completely gotten over them? I had an uncle who did what he could to support my brother, and yet my brother was already far away. My uncle had done the best he could.

In my life, however, everything was quiet at first. A great silence… I used to sleep for hours as soon as I got home from school. I always sleep when I can't cope with something. I understand it better now. So it was like this in the beginning, like the calm before the storm. Later, it all morphed into a feeling that descended heavily upon me. I would suddenly burst into tears in class. Many people did not understand me. Some thought they did, but I didn't see anyone who could really understand me. I couldn't listen to my father's song, I couldn't look at my father's picture. I remember when I first went to see my father in that place. That crowd there, crying children in their mothers' arms, old aunts and uncles… I still can't get them out of my head. I couldn't even look at my father's face because I was weeping my heart out. I wrapped my arms tightly around him, unable to let them loosen a bit. I remember how hard he tried not to shed tears. He brought us chocolate and fruit juice. I think it's the only chocolate I've ever eaten while crying.

While we were going through this, my little brother was unaware of what had happened. He thought my father had gone to work. He went to work at a place where he can't even make phone calls? How many mothers had to come up with similar lies and I wonder how many mothers are still telling such things to their children? Of course, my brother understood over time, but I am sure he chose to remain silent. He was silent like many others. My mother, on the other hand, lost her companion, with whom she lived alone in a foreign land for years. Even though she tried not to reveal anything to us, she was very upset. While she had to deal with her children's problems, she had to cope with the fact that her husband was in jail. On one hand she had fake friends who did not even knock on our door in my father's absence, and on the other hand, she had to wade through financial difficulties alone. I saw with my own eyes how this quiet woman turned into a tiger. I saw how she caught up with everything by herself. I saw what injustice did to my mother. She didn't let troubles crush her and us during the following 2 years. May Allah be pleased with my mother and all mothers who hold their family together like my mother. I hope my mother is also satisfied with me as her child.

Of course, things did not smoothly settle down after my father's return. On the first day, when I saw someone sleeping in the room, I forgot for a moment that it was my father. Let no child forget his father's presence at home!

In time, we returned to our old order. I am 19 years old now. If you ask if I have forgotten those hard days… I haven't forgotten them. I am sure that I will not be able to forget what was done to me, my family and thousands of families even after I die. Even though I see my father with me every day now, I still remember how cold fatherlessness felt. May Allah be pleased with those who included us in their prayers even though they were not able to physically stand by us.

My father, my family and I … Our heads have been high and always will be. May all families keep their heads high always! An oppressor cannot get away with cruelty and I hope the oppressed receive generous rewards in both worlds.

HARD DAYS

Written by: Gul Sena, 17

We must make our voices heard all around the world and tell everyone that we have been persecuted and that our rights were violated although we were right.

I don't know how to convey my perspective to you regarding these days when everyone had a lot of different sufferings. After July 15, my mother and father were expelled. I wasn't aware at that time that we were entering the darkest times of our lives. I thought everything would be okay soon, when my father got a new job. It was then that I grasped what it means to have a hard time making ends meet. I have Type 1 Diabetes and Celiac disease and it started to become more and more difficult for my family to buy what I needed for my health. My mother also had Type 1 diabetes like me and had to give up her own health just for me. Because we were both using the insulin pump and she had to stop using it since it was too costly to procure two at the same time.

Our family income dropped tremendously. Only my

father was working now and his workplace was really terrible in terms of conditions. He was trying to make a living in the dust and smoke in a factory. After learning that both my parents were expelled and lost their jobs, my grandfather started looking for a job for himself and started working as a watchman at a construction site. During this time, my father had already changed several jobs.

One day our doorbell rang. I answered it. Some man I didn't know was asking about my father. I said, with a child's mind, that he was staying here with us. After I told my parents about it, my father started to leave home much earlier and return late. On May 4, 2018, at 06:00 in the morning, the doorbell rang. My grandfather, working as a watchman at night shift, was not home. My grandmother was with us, not knowing what to do. She was in a lather and I had never seen her like that in my life. She was trying to open the outer door with the balcony key. We all panicked when the police came. My father could have run away from home, but he didn't. We opened the door and my father said to the police, "I'm sorry, it's our morning mood." My sister was telling me that cops were coming, but I thought she was joking. When I got to the corridor, I saw the police entering. There were too many of them. My grandmother was crying and shouting and she passed out. My father wanted my sister and me to take her to her house. As we brought her down to her apartment, she would run back to our house.

When I came back to our house, there was a mess all over the place. While the police were searching the house, they cluttered everything and turned it upside down. When the police first arrived, I had put my phone inside my pillow to hide it from the cops. One of the cops grabbed my bed and knocked it down but couldn't find my phone. But later, I took it and gave it to them with my own hands. They collected it and also took all the electronics stuff in the house. They found nothing in the house as evidence, but they still took my father into custody. When they told him to get ready, he fixed some clothes in a small bag and asked if any one of us had money on them. But unfortunately, none of us got any money. They took my father away just like that. We didn't know where they were taking him. My mom went to police stations all over the city and we finally found out where he was. My father stayed in detention for four days. Then he was arrested and taken to Bursa H-Type Closed Prison.

I was certainly experiencing a number of firsts in my life. I've never been to prison before but now I've been a frequent visitor. The guards in the prison were very rude. They were giving me a hard time as we got there for visits. They didn't want to let me in because I was using an insulin pump, which was causing alarms to beep when passing through the X-ray device. So we got a medical report, stating that it was necessary for my health, but they did not accept it. And for that reason, I always had to take off my insulin pump to be able to visit my father.

Getting into the prison for the visits was so tedious. First we stood in line to give our IDs. The earlier you are admitted into the prison, the longer you could see your relative. Our visits were early in the morning. Although they were slated to start at 08.30, we were rushing like in a competition with other families to get the first place and so were leaving the house at 06.00. There were months of winters and months of summers. The prison wardens couldn't care less about the people waiting outside for the visit, although it was freezing cold. Even if those waiting were old or young, female or male, nothing would change. They didn't even care about the little infants among the people. After visiting my father, we went running back home to catch up with school.

I would like to tell you about the 2016-17 school year. All private schools belonging to the Hizmet Movement were closed and most of them turned into state-owned Imam-Hatip schools. Unfortunately, my sister and I had to continue our education in one of these schools for a year. It was a place like hell. It was as if we were walking to death. The students were very rude, impudent and fearless. They were behaving very impolitely even against our teachers and used their phones without permission if they wanted to. Our teachers were like the embodiment of AKP. Sometimes they would interrupt classes and gather us in the Conference Hall, deliver speeches about the President, remind us of July 15, and then force us to applaud them. Afterwards, they would say, "Report or kill any FETÖ member you see". The schoolmates exaggeratedly repeated the slogans and hurled curse words. I was literally walking around school in fear of death. I wasn't talking to anyone. At the conferences, I was doing what I was told and clapping for the people on stage until my hands exploded.

Once, I was heavily beaten by my friends. I had to leave that school urgently. My father was with us at that time. We asked one of our relatives to use their address so we could change our school. They devoured that beautiful school in front of our eyes. I continued my education in a normal school. I am so grateful to those relatives for they helped us a lot and saved us from that hell when everyone else had turned away. I somehow finished secondary school by having to change schools a lot and eventually I was able to enroll in a qualified high school and continue my education there. No matter how much time has passed, I still remember the events we experienced like they happened yesterday. We must make our voices heard all around the world and tell everyone that we have been persecuted and that our rights were violated although we were right.

NEAR BUT FAR

Written by: Ebrar, 18

I desperately needed to be embraced, to be consoled with words like "Ebrar, our cause is the cause of truth. Don't worry, my Lord will treat you with ease and relief."

It has been almost 6 years. It's not easy to say. It was 2016 when my father was arrested. It was Friday, April 15th, at 6.45 am. Everyone was asleep. Of course, my father knew what was going to happen to him, but we did not know.

I don't remember exactly how many cops came to search the house, but I do remember my fear very well that day. I will never forget. My father was sitting on the edge of the sofa like a lamb waiting to go to slaughter. We witnessed the scene, as family members, as a police officer took my father's testimony while questioning him.

I have never seen my father so vulnerable before. "Dad," I said, "I will stay, I will stay here with you." But, my father refused. "No, you have school, you can't miss your classes," and he sent me away.

I went to school and took my seat. In shock from the events, I stared blankly and didn't hear anyone. Later, I and another friend whose father had also been taken into custody, were called into the Principal's office. The Principal sat with us and gave us a kind of pep talk. He said, "Ebrar, your father called me and entrusted you to me." So, after I left, they took my father away. I don't remember how much I cried at school that day.

If I am not wrong, it was 12 days before the transition test from primary to secondary education. I was in the 8th grade then. Days passed by with five hours of sleep everyday in order to win entrance into the science high school. I had very nice friends and my classes were good. I went to private school and I had high quality teachers. I feel deep gratitude for them since they would stay with us at after-school studies so we could go to better schools somewhere. Also, they would teach us how to be good people. Before I started the year, our college had an exam to divide students into classes according to their talents. I will never forget, the grade I got was 463 out of 500. I worked hard for a year. I tried very hard. I had scores close to perfect. But, come see that my Lord put us to this test of life.

My father was a math teacher. I don't remember making more than two mistakes in math tests during the year, and I almost always used to answer all questions correctly. But, after my father was arrested, I probably lost my confidence in mathematics. After he left, I couldn't score perfectly again, and most of my wrong answers in the high school transition test were in mathematics. I was very disappointed when the scores were announced. My father used to say, "Even if you achieve going to the science high school, I will take you to my own school and I will be your teacher." By the way, my father's school was the third best in the city. I used to answer him laughing, "Daddy, what's the matter, even if I force it, I wouldn't get a low enough score to come to your school." I would say, "The worst I can get will be the Anatolian high school." This Selçuk Anadolu was also the second best in Sivas. What can I say? When the scores were calculated, the average of a whole year was 463. I don't know, but, perhaps, the pain I felt during the high school placement exam suppressed the scores. At that time, the pain from my father's troubles was so severe that I didn't even have enough points for the worst high school.

Dear daddy! I had to go to the school which I once

despised. This time, my father was not even there. He occasionally said, "I couldn't be your teacher there, but I will definitely prepare you for the university exam." But unfortunately, my father could not do this either. I am 19 years old now. It's been a year since high school ended. I had a high school life full of traumas. I always looked with disgust at my teachers at school, the people walking around, and the people I was traveling with on the bus. "It's all because of you," I would say. I still wonder how people could be so heartless.

When I was in the 10th grade, my mother got breast cancer caused by her deep grief. My dear mother, who was my only support after my father left, got cancer. I have never seen my mother in this state, in my life; so pale and bedridden. Her left breast and lymph nodes, in her left armpit, were removed. These lymph nodes provide fluid circulation in the lymph channels passing through the arm. If these nodes are removed, the arm becomes completely edematous, which causes a lot of pain. Even in that state, my mother would get up saying "My children should not see me in bed like this", and she would cook and do the housework. She shouldn't use her arm lest it swell. But, since there was no one to help her at work, she always had to use it.

My mother always says, "Ebrar, God bless you, you

took care of me when I was sick, you became my little mother." I don't know if I was really able to take care of my mother that well, I don't know if I was able to relieve her troubles even a little bit. I was scared sometimes, deep in burning thoughts: "God, what will I do if something happens to my mother since my father is not with us. If something happens to her, I... How do I take care of my siblings, how can I support them?" Every night I would go and check her, saying "Mommy, are you okay?". May my Lord not test any mother with the grief of her child's death, and no child with the absence of her mother at a young age! Because, when a child is without a father, her mother takes care of her, but, when she does not have a mother, no one takes care of her. Of course, the Lord is with us. If no one else looks out for you, he will, but still desolation is a heavy trial.

The first year we didn't tell my father about my mother's cancer. Almost the entire prison knew about it, except my father. One day, one of the inmates who was jailed with similar allegations and who knew my mother's situation, told my father in the ward, "Give my name [be an informant], exit the prison and save yourself." When he repeated this twice, my father said, "So, you think I am crooked and tell me this. I will never do such a thing, with Allah's help." I believe the Lord has bestowed my mother to us both for the sake of this dialogue and with the prayers of all our oppressed older brothers and sisters in prison. Here, the process only took my mother's husband, her left breast and arm. After my father was expelled, we did not have any income. In this situation, it was his friends who took care of us. They would come every month and leave some money, asking "Sister, do you need anything?" God bless all! They protected us and helped us in many ways. May God protect them as well. My mother was only 37 years old. She became both a mother and a father for us. Even the doctor said, "How did it happen? What did you do to get so upset and become so sick?" Currently she is 61 percent disabled. Her arm is swollen, she cannot use it without constraint as she uses a very tight varicose vein glove and constantly suffers from intense pain.

My Siblings, also, suffered serious traumas after these events. I have two sisters and one brother. All of them experienced these events by interpreting them in their own way. My younger sister coped with this process by screaming and taking her anger out on others, and experienced a continuous longing for a father. When my father's prison friends got their freedom after serving their sentence, she would say "Why isn't my father coming out? I want my father. Tell my father's friends not to visit our house. All is well with them and their children are happy now for uniting with their fathers." She was in the 5th grade at that time, now she has grown into a 16-year-old big teenage girl. My other sister lived quietly in her inner world. She is such a mature girl that you can't say that this girl is 12 years old. My youngest sister was in first grade when my father left. Now she will be in 7th grade. My brother was five years old then. I think a boy needs a father more than a mother as he grows up. When a man showed affection, he would sit on his lap and would stay there. Perhaps he was in search of fatherly love. He would cling onto my father during the contact visits and he would never leave his lap. He would talk incessantly and never got tired of talking. My father used to always tell us, "He is your only brother and the youngest one among you. Do not beat him, do not be angry with him, always protect him". Those were the days when we were able to have contact visits. We have been longing to touch and hug each other for two years because of COVİD-19.

In February 2018, there was a very serious police raid. It was part of an operation involving 70-80 people from cities such as Kayseri and Tokat allegedly for financing terrorism. In this operation, my beloved mother was also detained after a house raid at 6.45 a.m. Those who experienced it will know what I am talking about. If the door is knocked on early in the morning, the whole household wakes up in fear, "Oh, the cops are here, they're going to take another one of us!" but, usually, it turns out that the neighbor rang the bell. Everyone exhales an "oh!" of relief and returns to their sleep. If the bell rang late at night, then there is excitement, not fear. The excitement of "Has our father come?" However, the neighbor again. She forgets the key and is left outside, so rings our bell. Again, everyone goes back to bed with a sad excitement.

Yes, my mother was also detained with this operation in Konya. I was 17 years old or would turn 17. I could do nothing. It's such a desperate situation... All you can do is pray "My God, let them go, please God, please." That day, they took our phones, the money my mother earned by making and selling vinegar, and my mother. They even seized the money in my youngest brother's pennybank, but we said, "We have no money for food, after this woman leaves, we will starve. At least, leave this money." Thanks to this gentleman, he took pity on us and left the little boy's money.

At that time, I was taking private lessons in physics and mathematics. That day, after my mother was detained, I went to my math class. I called my teacher before I went, but she didn't pick up. Anyway, I went to her house and we did the lesson. Before leaving, she told me "Ebrar, you know, your mother has just been taken, so be careful, don't talk to anyone for a while and let's take a break from our classes." She simply said, in a polite manner, "Ebrar, don't come again." Of course! The people of our region are so fond of leaving their companions in the middle of nowhere. I had physics class the next day. I went to my teacher's house and her mother-in-law opened the door. I was just about to say "Aunt, I had a physics lesson," she interjected, saying "Oh, my daughter, please go! I heard that your mother was taken into custody, it may happen to my daughter as well. So, please! Don't come again." These people have gone through the same thing as us, so you expect at least a bit of understanding, don't you? Unfortunately, the woman didn't even come out herself but instead had her mother-in-law say these things. Three years have already passed since this event, but I feel my heart is still broken. I even prayed "This sister chased me away from her door and may my Lord chase her away, too." I don't know, but maybe this was a heavy curse. Now, I say "May God give her a favor." At that time, I desperately needed to be embraced, to be consoled with words like "Ebrar, our cause is the cause of truth. Don't worry, my Lord will treat you with ease and relief." I don't know but maybe that's why my Lord sent me to her door that day, but they kicked me out of that door.

My mother stayed in detention for 3.5 days. She

says those were very difficult days. "There was a girl like a lioness. If it weren't for her upright stance, maybe, I would have given up my case for you," she said. It was ten hours, if I remember correctly, the interrogation started at night and finished in the morning. My mother was detained just for making and selling vinegar, just because she was cooking, and just because she used the words rice, curtains and medicine on the phone. The court of appeals upheld her sentence and now her case will be forwarded to the Supreme Court. She has been on trial for three years, without any crime. Of course, no one has committed any crime. My mother is being tried for innocence of having committed no crime.

After these events, even my own aunts stopped visiting us. People we once called sisters would either shunt or turn their eyes away when they came across us on the street. Neighbors would point their fingers at us and gossip among themselves about us. Ahhhh! What can I say? I'm a person who represses her feelings and endures grief in silence. I don't cry that much, but at the end of the day, we are human and the heart is hurt. After the university exam, I must have been psychologically overwhelmed, which my mother noticed. She took me to a doctor. I told you that I don't cry so much, however, I don't know why, but when the doctor asked what my problem was, all I could say was "Daddy..." and then I started crying. I went to a few more sessions and got some relief.

Later, my mother decided to send me abroad after a number of investigations into female college students in Turkey. While making my university preferences, my father was objecting to my selecting universities outside my hometown, saying "No. Whom will I trust? To whom will I send you?" Thank God, we received news from a sister that a university in South Africa was recruiting students. I told my father this and what he said to me was "My daughter, may your path be clear, may my Lord bless your migration!" This man did not send his daughter to a different city in his own country, but said "good luck" to South Africa, a continent away. Trust is such a thing.

Yeah. My name is Ebrar. I am 19 years old. It's been eight months since I came to South Africa. If my Lord wills, I hope I will learn English and become a math teacher like my father. My test in Turkey is over. Now, when the doorbell rings, I no longer think "Is this the police." I can use all the banned words and read the banned books here. All praise is due to Allah! I think I have only responded to my father's letters four or five times in five and a half years. Whenever I write, I always cry, my heart can't endure it.

You don't really understand how heavy the burden of the ordeal actually is while you are passing through it but when you start narrating it, you say "Oh... how did I experience all this?" Again, while I am writing this letter, my tears, which I wasn't able to shed comfortably in Turkey, started to flow just as I was writing the first word of the letter. I don't know if I won or lost my test. May my Lord not separate us, protect our brothers and sisters. Give our Hizmet life and strength, and let it not fail. May my Lord give our Teacher (Fethullah **Gülen**) physical and mental health and keep him presiding over us. While I am writing this letter, I wonder if I am competing with others in terms of whose troubles are bigger. May my Lord not let us compete with other people over troubles. May he not give us burdens that we cannot carry. One day, I don't know if that day will ever come... One day, I hope, with the permission of my Lord, we will return with a better and stronger Hizmet than before. I feel as if that day is so close and at the same time so distant as if it will never come. May my Lord keep the prayers and compassion of our prophet (PBUH) on us. Amen.

Stories of Hope

STARS TOO FAR AWAY FROM EACH OTHER

Written by: Osman, 10

"I believe much better days are waiting for us around the corner. Actually, there is a lot more to tell, but I don't want to be upset by thinking about them."

Hello, my name is Osman. I am ten years old. It has been 66 months since my father left home. They took him away in 2016. I was four years old. At that time, I was attending a kindergarten. I don't remember much about my father being taken away from home. We were sleeping when the cops came. The police woke up my sister and me to search our room. That's what my mom told me. The police took my father away. He didn't come again. I always thought that my father was teaching Mathematics in prison. But when I grew up and became cognizant, I learned this bitter truth. I learned exactly when I was seven years old that my father was in prison. I cried a lot.

A year after my father was taken away, my mother got sick. We learned that my mother had cancer. My mother had surgery and they removed her breast. After my mother had surgery, I got sick too. For two weeks I burned with a fever of 39 degrees. They couldn't bring my fever down. The doctor insisted that I be hospitalized, but my mother did not accept it because she had a new operation. They lowered my fever by giving antibiotics and serum in the morning and evening.

We hid my mother's illness and surgery from my father. After my father was sentenced to nine years in prison, during our first contact visit, I let him in on that "my mother had surgery and her breast was removed." When my father heard it, he was very sad and cried. When we got home, my mother said to me, "Son, why did you tell your father about my illness and surgery, you shouldn't give such gloomy news to a person in prison." And I said, "My father will not come anymore, that's why I told him." I had given up any hope regarding my father's return. All my father's friends knew about my mother's health condition, but my father did not. I wanted him to be informed, too. My father cried a lot in the ward. If I had then, the same reasoning I have now, I would never have talked about it. I didn't want my father to be sad and cry.

I gaze at the sky at night. One day I said to my mother, "Mom, look at the sky!" So I pointed to the most beautiful star with my finger and said, "Look mom, here is my dad!" I pointed to a distant star and said, "and this one is me, mom. We are as distant as these stars." I miss my father so much. I have such fancy dreams about my father's return. For example, I want to go to a nice hotel and sleep with my father. I want to go to the swimming pool of that hotel and swim with my father. I want to go watch a soccer game with my father. I want to walk hand in hand with him and eat ice cream. I want to wash our car with my father. I want to go on a vacation with my father.

A month ago, I was checking the court files of my parents. On my mother's file, there was a note "received by the archive of the Supreme Court of Appeals," and I also read "crime of terrorism." I said, "Mom, how could you be a terrorist? You don't know anything about weapons. If a gun makes a popping sound near you, you will faint right there." My mother also had tears in her eyes from laughing. I'm indeed used to being the son of a terrorist now. Neighbors see it that way. They say to me, "Your father is an infidel, once he comes out of prison and kills us, we will all be martyrs." But I know that my father, the best man in the world, performs daily prayers, reads the Qur'an, prays for everyone and rushes to help whoever is in need.

My father is also very handsome, with long hair. He solves math problems so well. His inmate friends told us that he rushes to the aid of everyone in the ward. He is the one who's been under detention the longest in the prison but God knows everything and he certainly knows about my father. My father prays for us so much.

I had a dream. In my dream, I saw our Prophet (PBUH) with my father's inmate friends. My father's friend took me to a mountain. We dug a spot there and took out four books. One of them was a big prayer booklet of Surah Yasin and the other was the Quran. We took those books to the mosque. When I went back to the mosque in the morning to look at those books, there were no books, but the sound of the Quran was coming from a room inside the mosque. I entered the room and I saw the Prophet (PBUH). He was reciting the Quran and his voice was beautiful.

When I woke up, I told my mother about the dream. My mom said, "Is it real?" She was very happy and cried a lot. "What was he like?" she said. I said, "The Prophet was dark-skinned. He had a beautiful voice and he was reading the Quran very well." We have had many events like this. I believe much better days are waiting for us around the corner. Actually, there is a lot more to tell, but I don't want to be upset by thinking about them.

Stay well…

Stories of Hope

GIFT CHEST

Written by: Mehmet, 11

"We buy gifts for my father and save them in a chest. When my father comes, he will open the chest himself."

Everything was so ordinary and beautiful that day. I would have never thought that my father would go. "He went to work," my mother said. I thought for an entire year that my father was away from us for work. But, then I learned the truth and was so upset that he was indeed away from us because he was a good person. Then I thought: I'm just separated from my father whereas he is separated from his sons and wife. That's why I recovered my senses and started behaving so as not to make my father sad anymore. I thought, "My father is far from me, this is true, but how can I stay strong in this situation?" I have to stay strong because if I look sad, then my brothers will be sad when they see me like that. Then my mother who sees us that way will be sad and finally my father who sees my mother that way... it continues in chains. That's why we should all stay strong and appreciate the value of having a family.

Even if you are separated from your brother, you start saying "I wish I had taken care of him a little more; I wish I had hugged him one more time. I wish, I wish, I wish…" It goes on like this. That's why we should cherish every moment. I for one have spent this time so well to improve myself and I did so always thinking of my father. English lessons, basketball training, swimming… and then the summer is over. Then you are in another whirl with the school, home, homework assignments… and the year is over before you know it. Over the years, I have improved myself. And I was always keeping my father updated about what I learned. Not just me, but my whole family.

Sometimes I really miss my father. Then I let myself into my room and say to everyone, "I'm daydreaming in my room, please don't disturb me!" Then I lie down on my bed and close my eyes. I'm in the hall. The doorbell rings. I open the door. It is my mother, and my father is standing right next to her just in front of me with a navy blue suitcase. He's wearing jeans and a white plaid shirt. He calls me "my baby" and hugs me. This may sound contrived to you, but it really works. Well, mostly… Sometimes it just doesn't. And then all I want is to cry. I cry because when you have pain, you have to experience your pain.

The worst is father's day and my father's birthday. Actually, I don't get very upset on birthdays because my father and I have the same birthday. I spend my birthday so happily that I don't have time to be sad. These days, we buy gifts for my father and save them in a chest. When my father comes, he will open the chest himself. We take a lot of photos and send them. And we also have a cat, who loves my father very much; He licks my father's photos and lies on his clothes. I stay away from it a bit because I am allergic. I also have an imaginary dog. One year old Belgian wolf, his name is Bolt. It's imaginary, but we're having a lot of fun. While all this was going on, four years passed. Two years left.

Maybe my father will come tomorrow, maybe even closer than tomorrow...

I WISH I DIDN'T KNOW

Written by: Zeynep

"I know my father is innocent. My father is there with honor. And one day everyone will find out that my father is innocent. I am proud of my father."

Think about it; You have a wonderful father who loves you very much, plays games with you, always makes you laugh and never makes you sad. Yes, my father was like that. He never got angry with me or my brother. He would joke with us and play games with us. Once, my father and I invented a game for ourselves. For some reason, we really enjoyed playing this game. The game was like this: we would turn off all the lights in the house except the living room. We wait in the living room for our father to hide. My father hides in one of the dark rooms and waits for us to come to find him. When we get close enough to where he is in one of the dark rooms, he suddenly gets up and says "Booo". For some reason we loved this game so much. My father, brother and I used to do exercises; not anymore, because I don't remember many of the moves. Yet, they wrongfully separated this wonderful father of mine from me. The day our father left was the worst day of my life. I'm sure the day he comes back will be the best day. It was a perfectly normal day. I went to school, came home, played with my friends on the street, but how could I have known that this would be the end?

While I was riding my bike on the street, my mother came up to me and said "put your bike back on, come right away." I put the bike in its place and headed back to where I talked to my mother just a moment ago. She wasn't there. Then I thought she went home. When I got home, she was there but I couldn't see my father's shoes. I was scared and wondered if something bad happened to my father. My mother was fussing around the house with tearful eyes. I wondered if someone died, so that my mother was crying like this. As I was trying to understand what was going on, my mother took me to my room, held my hands and said, "Someone slandered your father and me, but don't worry, we are not guilty and will be back in a few days." My mother indeed came a few days later, but it has been over two years and my father has not come.

I started crying as soon as my mom said the first sentence. But it wasn't like other cries because it didn't stop. I was sitting in the living room and my brother was watching TV there, unaware of everything. I've always envied him and I wish I hadn't been aware of anything! My mother was trying to comfort me but she was also running inside the house in a hurry. Then the doorbell rang. "Who is it?" my mother called. Someone responded, "carpet seller." He couldn't choose a better time. My mother opened the door and it was the police. What would have happened if my mother had not opened the door? Would they still forcefully break in? The police had come to detain my mother. As I recall, there were three or four policemen at the door and five police cars had parked around the building. After that day, whenever I see cops, I get scared, so I don't want to see them again.

My mother called them in while she retreated to her room to put on her hijab. She said she invited them so they wouldn't stay at the door. I wish they'd stayed! A policeman came to the door of the living room. Normally,

I am shy not to cry in front of people, but that day I cried without taking my eyes off that policeman. My brother said to the police, "Will my father come?" The police said, "Yes, he will." And yes, by the way, all of this was happening in front of my little brother. My grandmother arrived at 12 o'clock at night. My mother was planning to host some guests that night, so she had prepared some meals.

While my grandma and the others with her were eating, I tried to read a book. But I wasn't able to interest myself in it. I couldn't read at all. That book is still in my library. Even though I know I am already halfway, whenever I attempt to choose a new book to read and see that book, I skip it. Anyway, I went to bed. I guess I just wanted to get out of all of this hassle and relax. Just like the alias "He Who Must Not Be Named" for Lord Voldemort in Harry Potter, we call the day when these events happened "that day" and we directly understand what day we are talking about. The next day my uncles came. We closed the house and went to İstanbul with them.

I was reading "Oliver Twist" on the sofa. My aunt, speaking on the phone, and my uncle behind her walked in and kissed me on the cheek. "Your mother is coming," he said. Later, as I was preparing to go out to buy bread with my uncle, my mother came through the door. She took me in her arms and at that time, my uncle was consoling me saying "Your father will come too." I learned later that my father was tried on charges of "terrorism." But my father has a book about the Dardanelles War. How can a terrorist(!) write a book about the liberation of this homeland? We stayed with my uncle for a while, then with my aunt for a while, and at my grandmother's house for a while. My grandmother's house had only two bedrooms. So in the room where we slept, we also watched TV, ate, studied and my brother played with his toys. I started a new school in İzmit. I still miss my old school so much. My English teacher asked me twice what my father's job is. I said I didn't know. And every time he sneered and said "How can one not know where his father works?" and the whole class laughed at me.

I used to cry most nights when I was at my grandmother's house for hours. But now I realize that crying doesn't help at all. Because no matter how much I cried, my father was sentenced to eight years.

I have seen my father many times in my dreams since he left. In my first dream, I saw that my father was being released on April 21. I was so excited that he was coming out in just a couple of months. Then my mom came and said he would indeed be out on April 21, but after two years. I started to cry loudly as "daddy, daddy." Indeed, it came out later that the court date was set on April 21. In my second dream, we were on our way to visit a neighbor family as guests. As I was walking, my father suddenly appeared next to me; We hugged each other and started to cry. "I'm back," my father said. My third dream was the one that affected me the most. It was morning. My mom was standing by my bed and telling me to wake up and get ready. Then suddenly my father entered the room. I went towards him with tears in my eyes. I was saying, "Daddy, please be real. Please don't let this be a dream, but reality." Then I started to mumble "No, no, this is not true. My father cannot come." But, without knowing it was a dream, I convinced myself that my father had indeed come, and I ran to him and wrapped my arms around his neck tightly.

My father has been gone for two years and he will likely not come for another three years. I really miss him. Some think my father is guilty. They laugh and say, "If you are a criminal, then bow down to your fate. If you are innocent then say you are innocent." But I know my father is innocent. My father is there with honor. And one day everyone will find out that my father is innocent. I am proud of my father. He's the greatest dad in the world.

I LOVE HIM SO MUCH!

Stories of Hope

CLOSE FRIEND

Written by: Eylem

"This beautiful person, whom I call bro, taught me that even in the most difficult conditions, it is possible to be full of life and hope."

Hello, I'm Eylem. I would like to tell you what I have experienced in the last five years. Five years ago my mother was terminated from her teaching position by a statutory decree. From that point on, my life changed drastically.

One day while I was playing with my friends in the street I went home to get a drink of water. My mother and brother were crying. I immediately asked what had happened. Frankly, I wasn't completely upset by my mother's misfortune since I didn't understand what that meant at the time and kept playing outside. Schools opened two weeks later. My mom's students were asking where my mom was, and I had to lie to them all. It felt very bad.

Two years passed like this. On the eve of Eid-al-Adha in 2018, my brother was in an internship and my father was at work. I got up early and was doing something on the computer. The doorbell rang. Before I opened the door, I looked through the door hole and saw that they were police. At that moment I started crying. As soon as I opened the door, they asked about my mother. My mother went to the door. They said they had a complaint against her. I was crying in the living room and a policeman was trying to calm me down. He was the good cop. There was also the bad cop. "We don't promise that your mother will come back," he said, ignoring the fact that I was crying at that moment. There was no one home and so my mother asked the cops if I could come with them. The good cop muttered "we can do it if you don't have anyone else nearby to drop her", while the bad cop cut him off and said "We can't take a child, give it to the neighbor." Then they asked about my father, my mother said he wasn't here. The cops didn't care much about it.

While they were talking, I took my mother's phone to call my father when the police were gone. But when they saw the phone, they took it from me. When the police left, I went to our neighbor's house. I called my father on their phone and explained what had happened. Since the school where he worked was far from our house, my father could only come after 1-2 hours. He said he was going to the police station and I immediately objected. I was very afraid they would also take him in, but he left and came back an hour later. He said they didn't let him in the police station.

A little later, we received a phone call. An officer

informed us that they released my mother after questioning. I was so happy. We immediately went out to pick her up and met her on the road as she was walking towards us. When my mother came back, she was saying that a neighbor had filed a complaint, accusing her of membership in a crime organization. She was shouting inside the condo that she would find that person.

My mom said she wanted to move. I told her that I would not leave her alone, that I would go with her. We went to a nearby forest together and cried a lot. It was a neighbor in that building who complained about my mother. My father refused outright the idea of moving out. Events developed in a way that I did not understand. We moved to another house with my mother and my parents separated. I started another school. Since my mother was working, she left the house very early and came late in the evening. My only friend in those days was a cat. Over time, I made friends at school, but I couldn't tell them the truth about my life. It was very agonizing for me to give false answers to their questions. At the new house I played in the garden. The friends I grew up with were all far away. Good thing I had a cat.

Something nice happened at that time; A friend of my mother's was a guest in our house and that really brought joy to my life. She was a young girl who was only in her 20s. She stayed in prison for two years and she was released on probation, her case was pending. Despite everything, despite the pain she went through, she was full of life. When my mom was at work, we used to go to the movies after school. We would have a snack on the way back. Our ages were not close, but we were both terrified of the police. One day, on the way to the cinema, we got off the subway and saw the police surveilling the subway door. We held hands so they thought we were mother and daughter. She gripped my hand tightly like a clamp so that I will never forget that moment. I was only ten years old, but my best friend was a prisoner. This was very interesting for me. She was my best friend for a long time. We had so much fun together. It was teacher's day. We wanted to surprise my mother, who was working at the gas station at that time, with a cake we made ourselves. My mother was very happy. This beautiful person, whom I call bro, taught me that even in the most difficult conditions, it is possible to be full of life and hope.

There is no change in our terms yet, but we are a happy family. We all have dreams and goals. In the future, I aim to be a person with a cause, especially working on animal rights.

Stories of Hope

CHILDHOOD

Written by: Mehmet, 10

"Son, always set a goal in front of you, because if you don't have a goal, you can't be sure where you are standing and you don't know where you are heading to."

My father never appeared in court during the two years he was detained and is still in detention. I will never forget the day my father left. There was a knock on the door at 7 am on a Monday. I woke up right away. When my father opened the door, I heard three different voices. They went into the hall. I started listening to them from behind the door to understand what was going on. These three people were the police and one said, "Can we start searching the place if it is OK now?" When I heard this, I immediately ran to my bed and waited.

After a while, I heard some footsteps and the sound of a suitcase. When I jumped out of my bed and went out into the hallway, I saw a policeman holding handcuffs. Seeing that I was there he put the handcuffs back. I ran and hugged my father. My father leaned into my ear and said, "Son, look after your brothers well and do not upset them and your mother!" I became very emotional but didn't cry because I knew that if I cried, my mother and siblings would be upset. After my father left, according to my mother, I sat down completely silent for an hour. My mother told my teachers about what happened to make sure that there would be no problem at school. When I went to school, all my teachers and friends were gazing at me and my brother differently. I couldn't understand. And after about a week, those gazes changed into angry, resentful, indifferent, contemptuous stares. They treated us badly even though we had done nothing.

Unfortunately, this treatment was not only in the school. Our relatives, neighbors, even those we had never met were treating us badly. Maybe they were afraid of going through the same situation, because I couldn't think of any other reasonable explanation. I was getting quite angry about this and the best way for me to vent this anger became studying. And owing to this way of managing my anger, I managed to enter a decent school with a scholarship. Here, my teachers treated me well even though they knew about my father. I was very surprised and while all this was going on, the mid-term break arrived. My mother took us to see my father.

After driving 600 kilometers [375 miles], we waited from 4 am until 7 am to get into the prison. But being able to enter the prison didn't mean the rest would go smoothly. We went through a lot of security checkpoints. Just a couple of last security scans were left when my mother asked me to deposit money in my father's prison account. So I grabbed the money and started waiting in a queue. When it was my turn, the uncle there asked me what I wanted. I said I wanted to deposit money into my father's account. Then that uncle told me that I was too young to deal with money. I got very angry and replied, "I'm old enough to go through all this, but am I too young to put money on my dad's account?" When I said that, this man probably got upset and asked me for the necessary information. Leaving after having the job done, the man stopped me and said, "How old are you?" I said 10. Then he laughed and said, "Okay, go to your mother."

When I told my mother about this incident, she laughed and said "well done". We passed the eye scan and came to the waiting area. We were so excited, we couldn't stand still. So I took my brothers to the door where my father would come from. Five minutes later, the door opened. A lot of men started coming out from that door, but my father didn't appear. The man overseeing the door started to close it. Just as the door was about to be closed, he opened it again. It was my father. He appeared walking through the door with a bag in his hand. I have never been this happy in my entire life. We hugged and cried with all our power. And when it was time to go, my father said, "I can't look back when I'm leaving, because if I do,

I can't leave." We hugged for the last time and my dad walked through that door and headed to his ward. We walked outside. I went through the eye scan and passed the checkpoint but my mother was nowhere to be seen. It turned out later that she was stuck inside since the device couldn't recognize my mother's eye. I laughed a lot at that moment and I still laugh every time I remember it. We went straight back to school.

Every night we prayed for my father and his friends. After a while, my birthday came. My father sent me a watch with a note next to it that read, "Son, always set a goal in front of you, because if you don't have a goal, you can't be sure where you are standing and you don't know where you are heading." This sentence has had a profound effect on my life.

Months passed, and the day came when my father was due for his first hearing. It was Thursday and I didn't want to go to school that day. My mom sent me anyway. In the middle of the 6th class, the counselor called me to his room. My brother was also there. My brother and I looked at each other for a while, and the counselor said, "Your father is coming." I couldn't move at that moment. Then all of a sudden I got up and hugged my brother and started crying. My counselor teacher hugged us and cried along with us. I said I wanted to go home right away, but they wouldn't let me. I couldn't stay calm until the classes were over.

After school was dismissed, we ran home without wasting time. There I saw all of our relatives who had cut off all contact with us after my father's detention. I was very furious and refused to go in. My mother called out to me, "why don't you come in." I said "they haven't called us even once, nor have they asked about how we were handling the troubles after my father was snatched away. They weren't worried about our difficulties. Now they have come to the house because my father is coming. I don't want to see them." My mother responded: "They are your elders, what you do is wrong. Go, welcome them and kiss their hands." I did as she said and went downstairs and waited for my father's arrival. A taxi stopped at the beginning of the street, I ran at once and hugged my father. My cousins helped carry my father's bags. We ate, my father was very thin. He weighed 110 kilos [242 pounds] when he went to prison, and had dropped to 78 when he got back home. When our relatives left, the call for night prayer was recited and my father told us all to do ablutions to prepare for the prayer. Then he told us about the funny moments he had in the prison. In this process, I appreciated the value of my family and my life and started to give thanks every day.

AS WE FORGET GRIEF

Written by: Betul

"You can't understand how precious something is for you until you lose it. I've been reminding myself of this phrase so much for so long…"

It's been four and a half years since my father was wrongfully taken away from us.

I think we are used to this grief-stricken life now, we have normalized it or maybe it is only in our minds. Maybe we tried too hard for that.

I don't know why I'm writing this at 3:13 in the morning, but before I go to bed, I always think of my father. I pray for him and cry sometimes, like now.

How strange is it that the people around us are not aware of what we are going through? My closest ones don't know what I'm talking about, or maybe they don't want to mess with it. You know, you don't want to investigate the vulnerabilities of the people who are closest to you, it must be something like that.

But at least I would like to share my pain with my best friend, Zeynep. I don't know if she would support me, give me consolation for what we went through, how unfairly we were treated. Maybe that's why I'm avoiding talking about it.

At least I know how it feels to suddenly lose people you care about.

I miss my father so much, I wish he was with us right now. I wish I could hug him. I wish he would call me a "chubby" girl again! I used to get angry when he said that. But now I thirst after it. You can't understand how precious something is for you until you lose it. I've been reminding myself of this phrase so much for so long...

I don't know when this longing will end, but this must be what they call a test. Still I thank Allah for my situation seeing people who are in much worse situations than us.

Some of our friends that are passing through similar ordeals feel so troubled, so pessimistic and sad! When I ask them about how they are doing, the answers I receive remind me of what we went through and all the calamities that struck us. All these attest to the veracity of that wise remark, "Allah doesn't let snowfall on mountains more than they can sustain." Indeed no one is tested beyond their abilities; no one is loaded with burdens heavier than they can shoulder.

If I tell others about the travails I'm in, they won't believe me. Because we have hid our state so well that looking at us from the outside, nobody sees what is on the inside. And we have convinced ourselves that things are not as they are. Maybe that's how we survive. Volcanoes are erupting inside us, but we just move on by simply putting on an attitude and facial expression that we see fit on our faces, in our actions. Maybe this is how we forget the pain, the longing and the lack of what we need.

AGAINST PERSECUTION

Written by: Hamit

"When I looked at my friends at school, I felt more mature. The things they worry about seem so small and insignificant to me."

My father has been taken twice. It happened first on a Saturday morning. I was getting ready to go to prep school. While having breakfast, the doorbell rang. We were surprised at first, as it was not normal for somebody to come at such an early hour to our house. But then my mother went to the door. It was the police. They came in, showing their IDs, they said they were coming to arrest my father. My brother and I did not understand what was happening. It was the first time we had encountered such a thing. 5-6 male policemen entered and they immediately forced my father to sit in a chair and told him to wait there without moving. Then they started to search the house by recording it on camera.

Stories of Hope

They searched the whole house with my mother accompanying them. They confiscated any technological device or accessory from flash drives, to keyboard connection cables, phones, tablets and computers. My mother was working on a dissertation project for her graduation and told them that she wanted to save the work to an empty flash drive to back it up just in case before they took the computer away. But the cops did not accept this at all. My father said to the police: "This is not our hometown and we do not know anyone from here. How will my wife contact her family or friends to ask for help? At least, leave this old push-button phone, which is indeed a memory of my late father, and contains nothing special but his photographs," he said. The chief inspector said to my father: "We are here because of terrorism allegations against you and are acting accordingly. If I wanted to, I would tie you in reverse handcuffs and lay you on the ground," he said. "We don't treat you like terrorists would do, either," my mother said. In fact, after the house search was over, my mother even offered tea to the police, even inviting the police to breakfast. My mother was accompanying the police while trying to give my father moral support and at the same time she was telling me to set off for the course, saying "nothing will happen", and on top of all, she was trying to prepare clothes for my father.

My father asked permission to perform ablution. After he got ready, he said goodbye to us and left the house with the police. My mother took us out to the balcony and said "Wave to your father". We waved goodbye to my father. My mother said cheerfully as if nothing had happened so that we wouldn't be upset, "Your father will come back, you don't have to worry, come on, go to the park". After a while, I left my brother at home and went to the market with my mother. Borrowing a phone from someone we did not know at the bazaar we called our relatives and explained the situation. Some of our relatives came to see us that day. When I saw one of those relatives who was a father with his children, I felt very bad and went to my mother and cried.

A few months after he was in prison, they transferred my father to a city far from where we lived. Going to visit him became very difficult, both physically and spiritually. So, we were only going for contact visits. Taking the time of visit scheduled for my father into account, we were getting on the bus at 2 am and traveled for 7-8 hours, and then we had to wait until noon, sometimes at the bus station and sometimes in front of the prison. It was really challenging for us, but meeting my father was worth it. Before entering the prison for the visit, we went through an extensive search at least three times and we had our eyes scanned by the eye control device. The search left psychological problems especially for my brother. We would go inside and start waiting for my father to come. When my father came, my brother and I would immediately jump on my father's lap and hug him.

During the visit, we could not understand how quickly time could pass. My father used to bring us snacks such as chocolate and ice cream from inside, and these were incomparably more valuable to us than those in any grocery store. But later they prohibited it. As if their depriving our father of his kids was not enough, they also prevented his joy of being able to offer us something. They were stamping a seal on his arm so that my father would not run away. My mother used to kiss that seal every time and say: "This seal will be your salvation on the Sirat Bridge," that razor thin bridge between Hell and Heaven which every human must walk on the Day of Judgment]. Whenever we turned from the visit, we could not recover our senses for days.

The days that I was absent from school were too many and this situation was drawing attention, which made me sad. In fact, a friend of mine once asked me: "Why don't you attend any social events?" I couldn't say anything, because I couldn't tell anyone about my father's condition. Although we were hurt as a result of many events that I cannot describe here, these events taught us to be patient and resolute for the sake of Allah's consent. When I looked at my friends at school, I felt more mature. The things they worry about seem so small and insignificant to me.

SILENT SCREAM

Written by: Selim, 10

"One day my grandmother kicked us out of the house. We walked the streets all day. We walked for hours without knowing where."

I miss my father so much. I ask every week - Daddy, when will you come?

I seem to hear him say - I will be there with you soon, son.

But he still hasn't come. I have grown up; I am now 10 years old. Until 3 years ago, I couldn't even talk to people. I was afraid, I was feeling ashamed.

We were told to evacuate the house immediately. We did so, and then we waited on the street for a very long time, sitting without knowing what to do. The only solution was to move to my grandmother's. My grandmother didn't want us but still we started living in my grandmother's house. Most of the time, she yells at my mom and us, and gets angry. She is an angry person. She constantly asks my mother "Do I have to take care of you and your children?" My mother tells us not to be afraid, but she cries all the time. I was locking myself in a room and crying, wanting my father to come. I couldn't stop crying, weeping inwardly. After some time, I would open the door. One day I forgot to lock the door and my mom and sister found me while I was crying, hiding behind the sofa. "Everything will pass," they said, but they were also crying.

One day my grandmother kicked us out of the house. We walked the streets all day. We walked for hours without knowing where. Fortunately, my mother's uncle saw us and went crazy. He phoned my grandmother and then he went there and talked to her.

One day I asked my mother: Did you get kicked out of teaching because of us? My mother said "No". "Is it because of my father?" I asked. Because everyone was blaming my father. "Maybe, we'll talk about that when you get a little older," she said.

I was asking her when my father would be back home, and she would always say "soon". She always said soon, but it's been five years and he still hasn't come. I was confused and didn't trust anyone. I am 10 years old. Over time, my tears dried and I cried inside. When I was little, I knew he was in the military, and it remained that way. My father is still in the military...

I found a place on the way to school, where people wouldn't easily notice. This was my secret crying spot. I found a tree to talk to. When I told the trees what had happened and how I felt, they understood me without speaking. I used to see my friends on the way to school. Their father would take them by the hand and bring them to school, and I would think of my father who could not be with us for an unknown reason, and I would be sadly silent. Fathers were stroking their children's heads. In our house, my mother was doing this, but my mother was not my father. She would say "You are better off compared to those children that have no mother or father. You have to be thankful." Sometimes she doesn't understand me either.

One day, a boy from another class, whose name I don't know, saw me crying. I immediately wiped my tears. He asked me a lot of questions. I ran away.

I wish there were no schools. I didn't want to go to school. School was an unhappy place for me. I was feeling that I had to quit school and start working, dealing with business.

When I was a first grade student, my teacher used to say "don't you have a mouth, why don't you talk at all?" He called me "my pretzel". One day my teacher was talking to my mother, "Why is this boy so scared, like a wounded sparrow?" he said. I was not speaking at all. I heard them and I wanted to tell them that I knew how to speak, but…

My mother could not buy what we needed sometimes. Sometimes she said "we'll get it when your father comes." This was driving me crazy. As I am more grown up now, I know that being angry was a mistake.

I asked my mother and my elder sister: Why do people go to prison? They listed many things. So, which one is my father? My father was not with us for years.

After a long time, we met bir brother **Rüzgâr**. He bought me a bike that used to go like a jet. I named it the blue old man.

He was just taking us for a ride. I get excited when he takes us for a ride, my sister never gets excited. But I don't talk to brother **Rüzgâr** much either. I am afraid of people. He looks sad but makes his face look like he is happy. Traveling meant fun. Everything was different with us. I missed my father.

LONGING FOR FAMILY

Written by: Habibe, 14

"I wish I could hold your hands like you'll never leave again. I wish I could hug your neck, like I will never let go."

Hello, I'm Habibe. I am 14 years old. We weren't actually seeing each other much anyway, but on a March day, I literally broke up with my mom and dad. My longing has never abated ever since then, and it doesn't seem like it will. As I grew up, the longing for my mother and father was always with me and I always wondered about what a happy family atmosphere would look like. I lost my family because of the crimes my parents didn't commit.

Our first encounter with the police was in 2015. One day we went to the city of [I]. A friend of my father's was having an emotionally difficult time and my father wanted to be with him to support him. At first my mother was very angry with my father. "They're searching for you everywhere yet you want to go there?" she said. My father's answer was, "He was with me on every bad day of my life. Now I can't leave him alone when he needs me." My mother couldn't refute my father's argument. My mother would deliver a speech at our home city [T] one morning, so we set out at night and dropped my mother at the place of her meeting and went home. Once we got

Stories of Hope

home, everything was in shambles. That night, the police came to our house. If we had been at home, my parents would have been arrested that night. Their kindness and loyalty to their friend could be said to have saved their lives.

After this our landlord kicked us out of his house and we started staying at my father's friend's house. One day when my mother went home to get her clothes, the doorkeeper of our building called the police to report her arrival. The police surrounded my mother's car, searched the house and asked about my father's whereabouts. My mother was very scared and told the police that her husband went to visit his father, who was very sick. We survived that incident, too.

Then my mother, brother and I came to my mother's hometown M. I was in third grade then. My father was in Izmir. Then my grandfather, the pillar of our family, a very nice person who did not hurt even an ant, was arrested in 2017 on terrorism allegations. Then my mother was stained with a label of terrorist. My mother and brother had to go to [İ]. I had no grandfather, no mother, no father, and the joy of my life, my brother, was also gone. There was only my sick grandmother and I. I had to stay there for my school.

Three or four times I woke up with the cops around me. I was very scared the first time. They took me away from my grandmother. They asked questions about my mother and father. I answered what I could answer. What had my mother and father done to them? They came two or three more times, I'm used to it now. I used to go to visit my mother from time to time, but wasn't able to stay there for long as I had to come back for my school. When my grandfather left, we were alone with my grandmother. My grandmother always picked me up whenever I fell. While she herself was suffering from longing, she tried to console me.

When my grandfather left, all our relatives disappeared. There was only my grandmother and I. My grandmother is a primary school graduate, but she went to school with me again. If I was assigned to read a poem, she would come to school to watch me. She never left me alone. She was with me every moment. My grandmother had suddenly lost her child and her husband and so she was also very sad, but didn't show it to me. My grandfather came 10 months later, but the cops were after us every minute. I went to see my mother with difficulty; they were looking for my father everywhere; we had to escape the country.

Mom and Dad made a decision. We were going to

go to my father's friend. My father stayed at home and my mother, my five-year-old brother and I walked for an hour and a half in the pouring rain. We went to my father's friend and my father came in the evening. We stayed there for three or four days and we thought we were saved. Then we were placed in a house, but it turns out that the house was under surveillance. We didn't know about it. From there, I went back to [M] but my parents stayed there. Then we wanted to be close and my parents also came to [M]. And the worst day of my life happened.

It was 6 am in the morning, a day in March. The phone rang as if in a hurry, and bad news... I woke up to my grandmother's saying "wake up my daughter". I understood, and my grandmother said to me: "Get up, we're going to pick up your sister." I could say "my parents?", and she fell silent. I understood, my mother's home was now a prison. We set off right away. In front of me were the police, and beside them were my dear mother and father, who were looking at me innocently. My brother immediately hugged me. We were all crying. The cops knocked on the door at two in the night. They took my mother immediately. My little brother didn't understand what was going on. We took my brother, we came to our house with tears in our eyes.

The first night, my brother started to cry "I want my

mother". We fell asleep crying helplessly, not knowing what to do. I was devastated, but I had to stand strong. If I collapsed, my brother would collapse too. We used to go to [i] every month. It was my father's court day. My grandfather went to court to watch the trial. We were excited and I called my grandfather after the court was over. "I'll tell you when I come back," he said. I was still thinking that he would give good news. He came, his face was very sad. My brother was playing outside. We went in. My grandfather said to me, "Calm down". I got it, it was bad news. They sentenced my father 11 years and 3 months, and my mother 8 years and 1 month. I was 11 years old then. I would have to live this long time without a father. I was devastated, I was sobbing.

We went to [i] every month. In my brother's words, we were going to his mother's workplace every month. He always told himself the story that his family was away working hard to earn a lot of money so that we could live a good life together in the future. It's been two and a half years now. Contact visitations were canceled due to the COVID pandemic and my brother and I had never been to a closed visit before. So I said to my brother, "We will see them behind a glass so that your parents do not get sick". He started crying. "How can I stand it if I can't hug them," he said. I was helpless, what would I say? "But this is necessary for their health" I said. "I'm not sick," he replied. So I said, "A lot of people other than you are getting in there" and I convinced him with difficulty. The first meeting was very difficult, we cried. On the way out, I said to my brother, "Did you see my brother, isn't our mother very well?" I said. The relative of someone who was slandered like my mother heard this. They told her inmate about it during a phone call and she told my mother about it. My mother cried. We cried too when my mom told us. How painful it was.

We have been going to closed meetings for a year and a half, and during this time my grandmother and grandfather never saw their children. They buried their longing in their hearts and gave us their visitation rights because only two persons were allowed at a time. I understood what was happening, but my brother didn't understand yet. Maybe he understands, too, but doesn't say anything about it. Sometimes he cries and we are confused about what to say, how to soothe him. The other day, my brother's teacher asked him to write a poem about father's day. Reciting his poem, he was sobbing when he started reading the couplet "I wish I could hold your hands like you'll never leave again. / I wish I could hug your neck, like I will never let go." We couldn't help our tears, either. Sometimes he says "their parents are picking up my friends from the school, but me, my grandfather," he says. We can only say, "You are privileged, no one else's grandparents take them."

My mom always tells us: "Don't let your head bow out of sorrow or shame, we didn't do anything wrong. Our heads are high, our foreheads are open. It's not our fault." She is really right. They are there because they do good. I am proud of my mom and dad. My mother wrote in a letter the other day: "If I were asked what is the single place that you wouldn't want to be in, I would say prison, but look where I am right now. My daughter, our difference from them is that we are innocent." Those who arrested my parents and locked them in prison lost both this life and the next. But the innocent meek who were made to suffer here won the most important reward, the HEREAFTER.

EFFORT

Written by: Zeliha

"We achieved this success together as a family in such a period."

My father was a civil servant. Everything was fine and we had a regular life. We could go wherever we wanted and get what we wanted. My youngest brother was only three months old. One morning, while we were having a happy breakfast together, we learned that my father had been dismissed from his civil service position. At that time, I was little, so I was not very aware of things. But looking at my mom and dad's faces, I sensed that something was wrong. There was unrest in the house.

I asked my mother, and she tried to explain it to me in an appropriate language. It was a holiday soon, but the state did not want us to stay in that house, which was a lodging house, even for a very short time. They wanted us to leave our house immediately. Everything happened so suddenly and we had so many memories in that house. Wherever you look, a memory, an incident comes to your mind. We moved into our new home in about three days. Although the house looked nice at first, problems soon started.

Because we had been living in a house with a sea view in Güzelyalı, it was very difficult for all of us to move to a shantytown far away from everything. Although my father had so many friends in the old neighborhood we lived in, no one cared that we moved.

A lot of things had changed in our lives, but despite everything, life went on. My school changed. In the meantime, I started to memorize the Koran. Since there was no heating in our new house, we were using a stove.

In the midst of all the hardships, my father used to bring some wood pieces left on the rubbish to at least have a warm room in the house by keeping the fire in the stove alive for us. Since the stove was lit in only one room of the house, the other rooms were very cold during the winter months. Still, we were studying hard in those cold rooms without giving up. I was striving to memorize the Koran to become a hafiz during this period and I wanted to stay in the dormitory of the Koran school. But unfortunately, due to what happened to us, they did not allow me to stay in the dormitory.

Again, we did not give up. Our home was about half an hour distant from the Koran school and I had to walk this road twice a day, sometimes with my mother and sometimes with my father. Meanwhile, I had to keep up with my normal school studies as well. Both attending school and being a hafiz at the same time were very difficult. My mother was cooking on the stove, my father was collecting and selling waste materials from the garbage every day.

Since being a hafiz is a very difficult process, it normally takes about two years to complete it. But I managed to finish memorizing the Koran in a very short time of ten months, walking miles every day. The whole family simply didn't give up. There were twenty of us in the class where I was memorizing the Koran, but out of these twenty, only I was able to finish it. I applied to enter the competitions. In the first stage, I was ranked first in Izmir and by working harder, I became the winner of the Aegean Region in the next stage. No awards were given after these two competitions, which normally should have been given. There was one more competition left on my target and I completed it with the first place, I became the first in Turkey. A small gift was given after this success. But it wasn't the gift that mattered to us. In such a period, we achieved this success together as a family.

PISTACHIO FAMILY

Written by: Bahar 11

"I was a little luckier than my brother. My father had taken me to kindergarten, but my brother had never lived with my father."

I'm Bahar Eflal. When I was five years old, I had a very nice school, happy friends and always smiling mom and dad. One weekend, I felt fear and gloom at home and could not understand what or why. I remember my mother crying looking at my face and watching me, touching my sister in her belly. Since that day, my parents have almost never laughed. My mother and I went to the village first and then came my brother. But my father was not there.

While my mother, brother and I were living together, my father came. When my father came to our house, the gendarmerie uncles also came to our house and started to search the house. They looked everywhere, so I thought they were looking for my surprises. While the gendarmerie was leaving the house, I ran to one of them and hung on his jacket. I said, "Uncle, my parents are hiding their surprise under my brother's blanket under the sofa in our room." The uncles looked at each other and came back to our room and lifted the sofa. They laughed when they saw my chocolates under the blanket. Since our room was very small, my mother would put things there and give me a surprise when I cried once a day. I told the gendarmerie uncles not to look for my surprise, but they did and luckily they did not take them. They didn't touch my surprises, but they took my father from me.

Even though I was little at the time, I was scared and I understood. I ran to my room and I remember my mom, my brother and I hugging each other and crying. My mother said; "Daughter, we are going to see your father on Friday." We went to see my father on Friday, but my father was not in the garden. It was in a very closed place. It was a constricting place with no light. "Will my father come too?" I asked. When she replied "No, baby, he works here now", I asked again "when will my father come?". My mother said, "His manager did not give permission, he will come when he gets permission."

My brother, my mother and I moved from the village to the county, where I started primary school. My mother and brother were at home. My mother was now also a father. Besides, she was also struggling for my father. Mom, dad, we were always alone; We called ourselves the pistachio family, but my father had no shell. We were protecting him with our own shells. In fact, it was called the nuclear family [This is also translated as seed in Turkish, consumed as nuts like pistachios], but we called it like this because the shell of the pistachio is strong and has two wings. My mother was protecting us with one wing and my father with the other. My mother said, "Let's be patient, my daughter, Allah does not waste those who do righteous deeds." God has always protected us. We didn't have relatives, but we had very good friends.

I am now eleven years old. I have already started middle school, but my father has not seen me even once go to school. I wanted so badly for my friends from primary school to see my father, but it didn't happen. My brother was in kindergarten. I was a little luckier than my brother. My father had taken me to kindergarten, but my brother had never lived with my father. But I had dinner with my father, watched TV and walked. But my brother didn't even see my father. I thought about it from time to time, and there were many times that I felt sorry for my brother. The other day, while sitting on the balcony, the neighbor's son called his father, "Dad, Dad". My brother repeatedly asked my mother, "Mom, what did that boy say?" My mom said "dad", but my brother repeatedly asked. Finally, "Hmm! What does dad mean? Why doesn't my father live in our house, but the neighbors' fathers are at home?" My mother looked at me and said, "It's almost time, son," and once again sighed and hugged him.

Now that I'm older, I know my father didn't work there. Although my father was right and innocent, he was in prison. I understand now. My brother is now my age when my father left. I say: "My brother, our father is working, it's almost time to come." But my father lived in very good times, planted very good seeds, and the seeds sown are now sprouting. This week, my father's students **Rüveyda** and Rümeysa called me. They said "Bahar Eflal, we want to help you in your lessons". I felt bursting with happiness. Because my father said, "Daughter, I am here, but God will not waste you! We took care of someone's children, and of course someone will take care of you." My father was now right. Together, we started chasing the dreams we had in these difficult times.

Stories of Hope

I WILL BE FAIR WHEN I GROW UP

Written by: Halit, 12

"I want our lives to be normal now. People should not be slandered as terrorists unjustly."

I'm 12 years old and I started 6th grade. My father has been imprisoned for about 4.5 years now, where he was sentenced to eight years. I was at my father's trial which was held in a large gymnasium. There were 400 other people who were also wrongfully arrested like my father. I wanted my father to come home that day, but it didn't happen, which made me really sad. My father was taken to another prison in a different city. During this time my mother was being treated for cancer. My mother was sick and very upset, so we went to live with my grandmothers. Later, when the arrest warrant was issued for the spouses of both of my aunts, they also settled with my grandmothers. It was very crowded as everyone slept in one room, because there was nowhere else to sleep.

1.5 years after my father was arrested, we woke up early in the morning to learn that the police had raided my uncle's house to arrest my mother. From that day on, she had to hide, and could no longer visit my father, go to the hospital or go to other places. Our lives were shattered. My aunt and grandfather started taking me to visit my father.

My mother couldn't stand the hardships of living like a fugitive and decided to surrender. She came to me and explained why she wanted to do this. If she was arrested I would be able to visit my father, and that she had entrusted me to my aunt who would take good care of me. It was the worst day of my life and I was very scared and sad. The next day, my aunt, uncle, lawyer and mother went to the courthouse. My mother's interrogation ended towards the evening. My great-aunt took me to the courthouse so I could see my mother before the trial. I was younger then and ran to the courtroom to see her. When I entered, I heard that my mother had been released. This made me so happy and relieved that my fears subsided.

For the first time after a long while, my mother would finally be able to see my father. I went with her on the next visit a week later. My father was very happy to see my mother and I thought everything was fine, but on the way out, the officers surrounded my mother. There was an arrest warrant, and they wanted to take her by force. My mother was crying and did not accept what was happening. I couldn't understand what was going on, and I was scared. My mother entrusted me to her friend who was there with her and left. I told my great-aunt who was waiting outside, that they had taken my mother. My aunt couldn't believe it. After a while my mother called my aunt from the gendarmerie's phone and said, "They're taking me to the courthouse, come over there." We went there right away. My mother's procedures were over and thankfully they released her. Then my mother asked them to take us back to the prison since her belongings were still there, which they did.

Why did they release my mother? Probably because my mother was a cancer patient, my father was in prison, and I have a heart problem. This was substantiated in all the documents. The judge who listened to my mother was probably a good person and so he let her leave. Thousands of mothers like my mother are still separated from their children. I wonder who is taking care of them. Recently, they sentenced my mother to 6 years and 3 months. My father still has 7 months of his sentence remaining. I am eagerly awaiting his arrival as there is a lot I want to do with him.

I was in 1st grade when my father was arrested. When our teacher taught us how to write a petition, I immediately wrote a petition to my father's judge asking him to let my father go. My mother still keeps it...

I now attend the 6th grade and I want our life to return to normal now. People should not be unjustly slandered as terrorists. I will be fair when I grow up. I will demand an account of what has been done to myself, and my mother and father. After all, God sees what has happened to us. Justice will be served in the future.

EGE'S FORTUNES FROM SURAH VAKIA

Written by: Ege, 10

"I used to read the part of the Javshan prayer where it says, "O Lord, who saves the captives," for my father."

My name is Ege. I will now tell you the story of my life. I have been separated from my father who has been in prison for five years. He went when I was a small child. We have been visiting him over a period of five years. We had to wait at the door for hours and sometimes we would line up in front of the prison even before sunrise. The officers would then search all over us. I was just a little boy but still they wouldn't let me go with my mother at the search site, so I had to go to the men's section alone.

Then they would take a lot of people into a small room. Sometimes the weather was very hot and the room was very humid, but still we had to wait there for three hours and our feet hurt a lot. My mother was also very tired, yet she would put me on her shoulder so that I could breathe. One time my brother's foot was in a cast. I was small and my mom couldn't take both of us. We were almost crushed in the crowd. Finally, the door opened and we would run ahead. Sometimes my father would come early and I would run and jump on his neck. I liked the contact visits the most, because my father let us climb on him and he would turn us upside down. There are three of us and my father used to turn us all over his shoulder. He used to bring snacks from the canteen. When he asked, "What do you want from the canteen, son," I always said I wanted a dog. My mother was very afraid of animals but she got used to the Scottish cat a relative had given us.

I always recite Surah Vakia. One day we went to see my father and I recited the Vakia in front of the prison. There was a backhoe outside, working on the road. I really wanted to ride it. "Can the child ride?" my mother asked the operator uncle. "Sure," he said. He made me sit on the driving seat of the backhoe. Then when I got off, he put 10 TL in my pocket. I said "no need" but he said "take it". When we got to the car, I said, "Look, brother, I recited the Surah Vakia and my fortune has come. I used a ladle and also the uncle gave me money." My brother had also recited from the Koran, but not the Vakia. He also recited it. Before long, a friend of my mother's banged on the window. She gave him 10 TL because it was my brother's birthday. My brother also got his fortune because he read the Vakia.

I am playing a computer game. Everyone was getting a hero in the game but I couldn't get any. I was upset because of that. I got up at night and recited Vakia. I got a premium character that hasn't appeared for a year and none of my friends possessed. From then on, whenever I couldn't get a character I wanted in the game, I would wake up in the middle of the night for the tahajjud prayer and ask for this character. In the middle of the night, my mother would wake up and suddenly see me, she was frightened.

My father would say, "Son, recite this surah for me too, so I can get out of here". I used to read the part of the Javshan prayer where it says "O Lord, who saves the captives," for my father. I was seven then. We also had friends who were separated from their father like us. We would go on a picnic with them and have a lot of fun. Some days we would meet and play nice games. My parents used to prepare surprises for us, and we would play together during the holidays.

My father had been sent to prison before I even started school. I'm in 3rd grade right now. I went to one of the visits with my school uniform on so that my father could see me in it. My father's prison was so far away, so we couldn't see him very often. We had to travel for seven hours by bus. I was usually very tired, but at the same time

Stories of Hope

I was very happy to see my father. My mother's friend brought me once because my mother was sick. I spoke to my father alone. My father said, "Son, how could you come here all alone?" Every time he saw me, my father would say, "Get back a little and let me take a look at you to see how much you have grown." Sometimes I would hide under the table. After my mother had talked for a while, I would suddenly come out from under the table and my father would look very surprised. We used to make biscuit cake every Friday with my father and I would love to do it again. He made up a (perfect 😊) cake recipe inside. My father said, "We will do this when I get out"

The prison where my father is can be seen from the balcony of the house we moved to. I wave at him: "Come soon, Dad." I said the tallest building is ours. He would come running. The house is close to the prison now. We already sold our car. My mother puts me on the back of the bike and takes me to prison. She picked me up from school again this week. We didn't tell my teacher where we were going. I just started this school. I said, "What will I say if they ask about my mother and father?" My mother said, "I talked to your teacher, he will not ask, relax". Since I haven't seen my father for two months, I did most of the talking. My mother was just about to pick up the phone, something was coming up on my mind and

I was picking it up again. And then our time was up and we said goodbye. I waved until my father walked away through the door. I wish we had never parted, as I miss him so much. 11 months left. I will meet my father in the summer...

NORTH STARS

Written by: Simal

"...don't let them take your colors and bury your soul in black and white, please don't let them shut you up. Defend yourself, never be silent."

Hello;

I am writing these lines for you on my bed in my modest room that cannot see the northern lights although I want to see them very much. Where should I start? What should I say? Believe me, I have no idea about this subject.

In fact, these things, which are very sad to some, always seemed normal to me. I don't know for sure why, but I have an idea. I think the reason things seemed normal to me was that I always thought there are people worse off than me. As a child I used to think, "I wonder if God hates me, if he does, why does he hate me? What have I done to him?" I was just happy. Maybe that's what he didn't want. The happiness of people, especially that of little children... Maybe just because of this, he took my father from me; the person I valued most in this life. Maybe God didn't love us like in fairy tales or as my family told me.

Another reason why I was able to normalize all the miseries was that growing up among the history books, I was already aware even at the age of five how bad a place the world was. I would think to myself throughout history God hated us, why would anything change now? According to what I learned from those books that were read to me and from the books I read, babies, children, the elderly, innocent people that had not committed any crimes at all, and the best mothers in the world were tortured and murdered. This happened just because of some stupid people's interests and racism.

I realized this fact long before I was separated from my father. I have just thought of another reason why I'm never sad in the face of these things. I think the main reason was not to give in to those who wanted to upset us, which is what they wanted. I never shed a tear because my father was there, and I knew that in a war the winner is the side that gets what it wants. I never cried so as not to let them win. And I'm still not crying. I swear I will not give the other side what they want, so as not to lose the war, until this little world on which we set foot stops revolving. Anyway, now you're going to read a lot of memories in this book, and most of them will be sad. Here are the memories of Şimal, who you will see if you turn your back to the south. Yes, now you know my name, I am Şimal. My name is of Arabic origin and means "north". If you are ready, I will start from the beginning.

It all started when I was 8 years old, that is, in the third grade. I still remember that day like it was yesterday. I was very sick that night and my fever had risen to forty degrees Celsius [104 Fahrenheit]. Even in the morning I was in an extremely bad condition. My father had waited by the side of my bed all night. At 11:46 the doorbell rang. I didn't know who it was, or my mother thought so. While my father was putting the cloth dipped in cold water on my forehead, my mother came in and they went out of the room together. When they came back a few minutes later, my father was hastily packing his clothes in a small travel bag. The last words he said to me before the bars came between us were "I'll be back, daughter." Then they took him. I tried to stand up to go to my mother, but at that moment I found myself on the ground.

My mother later informed me after four months that my father was in prison, and my response was to say, "I already know" and to continue eating. Well, you wonder how I knew? I was an extremely curious child and during the first month, I had already learned everything and even found my father's photo in the newspaper. I convinced my mother that I didn't know how to delete my browsing history. I had eavesdropped on her conversations with her friends and did a lot of research on these conversations on the internet. The reason I convinced my mom that I couldn't delete the browsing history was because I was wondering when she'd tell me, and as I said she divulged it four months later.

Oh, and wonderful people have entered my life. Maybe she'll not like it if I give her name here. Therefore, in this letter, I will address her with the initials of her name and surname, H.Y. She is one of the best, most wonderful, sweetest and most compassionate people I have ever met in my life. If my mother was not my mother and I could choose my own mother, I would want either anyone of my two little aunts or H.Y to be my mother. Oh, by the way, don't think I don't like my mother. I love my mother, after all, she is my mother. Also, I'm sure she loves me and my brother a lot.

Well, I'm going to talk just casually now. How are you beautiful people? You don't mind those who judge you just because you are yourself and then imprison you in a flat life that consists only black and white after cleansing all your colors and emptying your brain, do you? I don't mind them at all. I don't think you should either, because usually people just goof off. Throughout history, we have always been mingled with bad people, but we must not always keep in mind that those who wanted to imprison us in a colorless world were once colored. Once their colors were wiped off and their brains were emptied, they were implanted with a belief that they must consider nothing but their own interests. Every child is one day forced to lose their colors, and that's what people call growing up: turning away from their colors. No one knows what will happen in the future, but they most likely want to steal your colors too. Nonetheless, please don't let them, good people, because life is not worth living in black and white.

You only come to this life once. So paint your life with any color you like! Don't let people trap your soul and make you lose all your hues and turn into some bland black and white. Shatter the bars ahead, grasp that brush from them and paint as you like. Live with the colors you want, dance, sing, cry loud, laugh and discover yourself with clamorous sounds. Seek happiness near, not far away, don't let them take your colors and bury your soul in black and white. Please don't let them shut you up! Defend yourself, never be silent. I don't know where you are now, what you are doing, but I hope you still live with your colors. Stay with the colors, beautiful person.

With Love From The Direction The Brightest Star Shines In The Sky...

LOVE OF FATHER

Written by: Mehmet, 13

"Let's hope that no child grows up without parental love, grows up without a father when he has a father, and is always happy..."

In the dark of the night, a knock on the door...

-Is your husband here?

- (yawning) Yeah, who are you?

- We're the police, we're here to detain him.

My mother was stunned, speechless, unable to say anything. The cops came in, took my father and left.

It took two minutes for my mother, who was left standing where she was in the shock of the moment, to realize what had happened. And the question that would be asked for years to come was asked for the first time: "Where did my father go, mom?"

My mother turned to us, her eyes filled with tears and

she was about to cry. "Harvest time for olives arrived, your grandparents called and so your father went to help them," she said, as casually as she could pretend. We kids who were already sleepy - there were 3 of us - went back to our beds and continued to sleep. Yes, now that I've summarized the event, we can move on to what happened next. I, Mehmet, am the eldest of three children and I am 13 years old now. I was about seven years old when this happened and it took me until I was 11 years old to find out where my father actually went.

Frankly, I was very upset when I learned the truth. But we are human after all, we tend to quickly forget the intensity of our feelings. Also, my father was a manager. Of course, it wouldn't be normal for my father to stay out while all his friends, who were working under his supervision, were in prison. If one day they say, "We were all taken in but you weren't," my father would certainly be very embarrassed. Now he is beyond reproach. He will be able to say, "I also had to endure the test of treading on the path of the righteous as well."

I've been through a lot in my father's absence, but one of the worst was that whenever I saw a father and son in the park, I couldn't help but feel envious and sad. I always wanted to ask my mother again and again the questions that I knew the answer to: "Why is my father absent? When will he come? Why can't we have fun while other people are having fun with their dads?" Actually, the concept of "fatherly love" seems a little strange right now. As I said, people forget quickly, whether they want to or not.

Another thing that upsets me a lot is that our father cannot be with us in our important moments. For instance, I am acting on stage in a play and my eyes are searching in vain for my father across the audience seats. Or, I receive a medal from some competition and I am terribly in need of showing off to my father proudly; I come home but he won't be there. Yes, I wrote this last sentence with a slight smile.

Stuff like this happens a lot in everyday life. My siblings are still unaware of what exactly happened, because my mother always comes up with reasonable excuses to explain about my father's whereabouts. In fact, the olive harvest story expired after a while and then my mother started telling us that our father had indeed found a decent job at some distant place and that he is working hard to earn money and sending it to us so that we can live well here. It was because of his toil that we were able to live comfortably, she told us. My brothers are buying these stories, since they are still small kids. On each birthday, my mother gives two presents and says "this one is from your father".

As things went on like this, at some point, I naturally learned the truth and I started to think about my mother's feelings. For example, none of us had ever seen my mother cry. To us, my mother has always been smiling and playful and she constantly demands that we do our homework. I've never seen my mother cry. She once took us all to a psychologist to help us smoothly get through this process. Even the doctor said, "You are doing very well, keep it up." We are taking lessons to learn how to play piano and saz (a traditional Turkish musical instrument). We even attended a show as mother and son played saz together; it is a very good memory for me. Anyway, enough talking about my mom, let's get back to me again.

As I said, being without a father is very difficult at first. One of the other things I feel sad about is that, when everyone in the class is talking about their father and when it is my turn, I am not able to say anything. I'm always making something up. We didn't tell the truth to anyone. My father is sometimes a computer engineer and sometimes a teacher, but I always say "he is working away". One of the worst things about it is that I will forget my father over time. For example, I found it hard to accept when my younger brother once asked "Mom, what was my dad like?" Just as I was about to rebuke him saying "how can you forget him," I realized that I could also hardly remember the memories I had with him. They were very small when my father left, in fact my brother had just been weaned and he has no memory of my father in our house.

Let me tell you about an incident that happened to me recently. I love to play chess, and I remember more or less playing with my father when I was little. Anyway, there was an online chess tournament recently and I came 2nd in my city. I would like to show this to my father and say, "Look, I'm good at chess now, let me beat you as well". When I was little, I could never beat my father at chess. I mean, being without a father is not very sad at first, but as time passes, people want to see and experience the concept called "father's love" in their life. Let's hope that no child grows up without parental love or grows up without his father, and is always happy.

DAD'S SHOES

Written by: Ali

"A father should teach a kid how to ride a bicycle, not others."

I was very young when my father left. I wasn't even going to school.

According to my mother, I grew up on the roads. My father found a job a little far from us and works there. It's been a very long time and I guess he can't find our house if he decides to come back some day. My older sister says "My father used to live in this house, so he can surely find it," but I don't remember those days.

One day I went to see my father while my brother and sister were at school. I always see my father sitting behind the glass. I said to my sister, "My father has no shoes, this is why he can't come home." She laughed a lot. She mocked me saying "how can something like that be true?" I asked my father at our very next visit, "Dad, can you show me your shoes?" He was surprised, he lifted his foot up, I saw through the window he had shoes and I was very disappointed that day. I said to my father, "If you have shoes, why don't you come to our house?" He looked at my mother, surprised. They both bowed their heads and were silent. So I kept silent and gave the phone to my mother. So it wasn't the shoes that were the problem, but my father still hasn't come home.

I've made some really good friends here where we just moved. They love me so much. They always ask me about my father. I said, "Daddy is working". They did not believe it. "Our father also works, but he comes home in the evening, and we have dinner together, we watch movies together," they said. I asked my mother and she said, "Your father works far away, and if he comes home in the evening, he has to get up very early. There is no bus that goes there at that hour, what's more, he may be sleepy and his boss gets angry with him." I believed it, because mothers don't lie. My friends haven't even asked about my father for a long time now. No, we're all used to this situation.

When I go to see my father, the brothers there love me very much. They always give me something. They gave me a rose made of pearls for my birthday.

Due to the pandemic, we couldn't hug my father for a long time, we couldn't fight. My father used to wrestle with us. He used to buy the foods we loved and feed us with his hands. I love pistachios the most because my father opens it with his hand and puts it in our mouths. Eating something from his hand is an indescribable happiness.

I don't like seeing him through the glass at all. You can't touch, you can't hug and kiss. We play rock-paper-scissors from the glass, but even that is not so joyful.

I'm saving money now. The other day, my mother said, "What are you going to do with all that money? Buy toys and play." So I said to her, "I'm going to buy the place where my father works." My mother was surprised. "Why is that?" she said. I said "I'm going to be my father's boss and will tell him, 'You're done, you can go home now', and he will come to our house. So I need to save some more money, I can't spend it."

I pray every night that "all fathers finish their work and go home immediately." I don't like traveling at all, so we leave early, but I get very nauseous in the car. I no longer want to see my father at work, but at home when I come home from school.

I think all parents should be with their children. No one should separate us from our parents.

"A father should teach a kid how to ride a bicycle, not others."

THE LIFE IS BEAUTIFUL

Written by: Eda, 12
"Good people always win, we will win too..."

It was a Saturday. I was very excited about moving to a new city. Our home was beautiful and we loved our new home. We lived with my mother, father and three siblings. My mother got a job at the school we were attending. We used to leave the house together in the morning. But my father stayed at home, as he took care of my little brother. This was very interesting, because my father always went to work and my mother looked after us. This was something strange, but we didn't push it too hard, because we were happy. I signed up for first grade in the city where we just moved. Our school was opening earlier than the official start of the semester so that we could get used to it. Then my father said he wanted to talk to us one evening. "I have to go to help my grandparents," he said, looking into our eyes. He was going to pick olives. He even said to me, "Eda, you like green olives, right? I'll collect a lot of olives for you, okay?" He hugged us, kissed and smelled us. In the morning we went to school. When we came back, my father was gone.

My father had been gone for a month. We could only talk to him on the phone for 10 minutes. We had to wait 15 days to hear his voice. His phone was at home. He was calling us from another number. I was very curious about this, but I never talked to my mother about it. Later, my grandfather and grandmother moved to us and we started living together. Once my brother scolded me, saying "My father left because of you, if you didn't like green olives, he wouldn't have gone to pick them, look, he still hasn't come." I was very upset about this and I haven't eaten olives for five years. I will eat olives when my father comes back. I thought my grandparents came for a trip, but they are still with us, they did not go back. My mother said, "The olive picking work is finished, your father found another job in another city, he will work there from now on. If you want, we can go to see him once a month but we can only talk for 10 minutes, they're busy," she said. I didn't know if I should be happy or sad at that moment.

A month passed and we went to see my father. My mother always told us about it on the way. She said, "It's a little different there, it's fun like a maze, they're going to search us, scan our eyes, go through a few doors." So it turned out that my father was on a covert mission. This is why they searched us quite thoroughly to make sure that we were not bringing in any phones. Finally my father came and we gave each other big hugs. He bit my nose and sniffed me, brought us a lot of food and fed us with his hands. This visit passed very quickly. The brothers in charge shouted, "The meeting is over." My mother said, "Come on guys, let's go, let your father get back to work" and we left. Some children cried a lot after their fathers. They knocked on the door, shouting "Daddy come!" But no one opened the door. It's been such a long time and my father has never seen me in a school uniform. I am going to 6th grade now. I'm aware of some things, but I don't ask my mom so she won't be upset.

We couldn't go to see my father for some time

because of the pandemic. My father has the coronavirus. They didn't take us there as a precaution, but my father recovered quickly because I prayed for him a lot. My brothers also pray for my father a lot.

One day, our teacher asked our father's profession and phone number in the classroom. I couldn't tell he was undercover. I said, "He works remotely, teacher, and I don't know his phone number either." He laughed at me, saying "how come someone doesn't know his father's number?" But I knew the truth. It should have remained secret. I didn't mind them laughing at me. I was just a little sad, that's all.

Then everything was forgotten. Years passed. I have grown up. My father still works remotely. Only some little business left for him to attend and so he'll be back soon. Now I look forward to my father's arrival, so that my mother will no longer be upset and I will be able to ask my father everything that I could not ask her. My mother took care of us a lot and did everything we asked of her. She took us to courses, took us to the movies and she participated in all our programs. She is still struggling so much that we have not missed anything.

One day I heard my mother talking with someone. I heard her say that some nights, while my father was sleeping, some people were breaking into his room without any notice and searching it. My mother was very upset about this. Who knows what my father is doing now? He misses us so much, and we miss him so much too.

I graduated, participated in competitions, but my father could not see any of them. His heart is with us. Life can be cruel and unfair sometimes, but we should not be offended by life. My mother taught us this. It is very important to enjoy the moment, no more or less. Because time passes and we grow. My father will come home and we will go back to our happy old days. We will never part again, because God knows, my father is very good, he cannot harm anyone. Good people always win, we will win too...

DON'T SEND ME ANYWHERE ELSE AGAIN

Written by: Murat, 9

"I asked if we were also going to be like that when we grow up"

Hello, I'm Murat, and I am 9 years old now. In June 2019, my grandmother and aunt came to our house as guests. That day we played games with my cousins and brother, and went to the park. We had a beautiful day and I slept very happily that night. When I woke up in the morning,

Stories of Hope

my mother, father and brother were not there. At night, while I was sleeping, the police came to our house and took my mother and father away. My brother cried a lot because he was little, so my mother took him with her. When I woke up in the morning, I searched all the rooms thoroughly in the hope of finding them. I couldn't find them and then I started crying. My grandmother and aunt were trying to silence me, but I kept on crying. They said that my brother was sick during the night and they had taken him to the hospital. I waited for several days but they did not return. Being away from my parents and brother made me feel very sad and I was also feeling bitter towards people.

Three days later my journey began, when my aunt came to İstanbul to pick me up. After staying with me in our house for three days, she took me to the city where she lived. I took the bus ride with my aunt and cousin but I felt very sad during the entire trip. I was constantly thinking of my parents. It was my first time going to my aunt's house. Before leaving, she asked me about the toys I liked the most and she put them in my bag. When we got to their home, we played games with my cousins, who treated me very well. They shared their toys, but I was not happy. Whenever I asked about my parents, my aunt said that "They got a job, and will work for a while".

My mom and dad started calling me on the phone, and I couldn't help crying when I heard their voices. I kept asking when they would call again. My aunts took me for a walk, took me to the football field, did everything I loved to do to make me happy, but I could not be happy at all. My aunt used to take pictures of me and send them to my parents. I learned to read and write that year, and wrote my first letter to my mom and dad. My mom and dad told me on the phone that they were very happy. I was very happy too. When my brother saw my photos, he cried a lot saying how much he missed me. So my mother had to send my brother to me because he was bored inside where my mom was.

I was very happy after I received the news that I would be reuniting with my brother, and jumped up and down with excitement. We were ready to welcome him at the hour he was supposed to come, and when the bell rang, my excitement peaked. When my brother saw me, he jumped on me shouting "brother" and we both fell to the ground. It was indeed a very funny scene. We all laughed a lot even though I didn't have my mother and father, I was very happy that at least my brother was with me now. My brother didn't tell me the truth either, he said my parents were working and they would come later. After staying at my aunt's for a while, we went to live with my great-aunt and grandma. After staying there a while, we went to my grandmother's [my mother's mother]. Everyone took care of us, but my brother and I kept thinking about our parents, who we missed so much.

After a stay at my grandmother's, we finally went to visit my parents. I was going to see them for the first time in three months, and I was so excited. The place we went to was a prison and our time was limited, but I believed that they were working there. When my brother and I saw my mother, we cried and hugged her, and we didn't want to let go. She said we would see my father after her time was up. My mother left us, and we were crying a lot, then my father came and we never got off his lap. My father told us nice things. "Your mother will come tomorrow," he said. We cried a lot when we had to leave my father. My grandmother took us to our house. The next day, my mother was really out and our relatives took us to pick her up. My mother got into the car with her belongings in her hands and we came home together. My brother and I have never left my mother's side. I cried a lot, continuously demanding that my mother never send me somewhere else again.

We started going back and forth to visit my father. I now knew that it was a prison and I kept asking why my father was there. My mother told me one day that innocent people can go to prison too. I was really sad. "Are we going to be like this when we grow up?" I asked this because my father is a very good person. who treated everyone very well. We are now waiting to meet my father. I really miss him and I pray that the process is over.

FEELINGS

Written by: Tugba, 12

"After all that happened, I almost lost control of my feelings. I could be nervous and angry, excited and happy at the same time."

Hello, I'm Tuana. I am 12 years old. The events that I am going to describe now are not from a book, a newspaper, a magazine or a dream. All of these events are real, because I have experienced them. Well, let me start telling my story.

When I was four or five years old, my father had a very good job at a very decent school. We used to go to school together with him in the morning. I would go to kindergarten and my father would go to his room. After my classes were over, I would go to my father's room, where he had a small closet to serve guests. As soon as I entered the room, I would open the door of the closet, grab some snacks and soda and wait for my father to show up. Sometimes, I would go out to the garden and play to my heart's content.

Just as I was about to start 1st grade at the school, where I could run and play freely, and loved so much, our school was closed in a way that as students we could not comprehend. My father became unemployed and started looking for a job in other places. He even went to unload coal trucks several times. He would come back home all in black. Later we heard that my father and mother had been labeled as terrorists. My mother, brother and I went to my mother's village. A few weeks later, the gendarmes arrived in the village and my mother immediately hid in the barn, but the gendarmes found her and wanted to know where my father was. They searched the two-story house, even the roof, and took my aunt's computer, flash drives, even my grandmother's phone. I had to study the 2nd semester of the 1st grade in the village, separated from my mother, father and brother.

After the 1st grade was over, we came back to İstanbul during the summer vacation. We would be together now. We rented a small house next to a park. It was a makeshift old house, and its facilities were very poor, but it was nice to be together. One day, while he was visiting his friend's house, the police followed my father and took him into custody. My mother, brother and I were at home. The police came and picked us up, took us to the hospital, where they brought us to the police station after getting a medical report. The female police officer took us to a room,and gave me pen and paper. I drew a cup set, but I don't think those cops deserved it, because they tore our family apart. Then I went out of the room with my mother.

I was very afraid, being both motherless and fatherless scared me. Then my father's friend and his wife took my brother and I and brought us to my mother's uncle. They said it was 3:00 in the morning and from there, we went to my grandmother's house but by the time we got there, it was 04:00 am and I couldn't sleep until that night, continuously sobbing. A week later they let my mother go, but my father was arrested. I was really sad. On the one hand, I was angry, but at least we were all at a certain place and my mother was with us now. I couldn't be happy while my mother, father and brother were not with me.

Together with my mother, we went back to the city where my father was jailed. Every time we went to visit my father, he would buy us snacks. We used to sing with him and tell each other riddles. I was now in 3rd grade. One day, they took my father to another city without informing anyone. The road to the city where my father was transferred was very winding and dangerous. Our stomachs would turn upside down until we reached my father. That's why sometimes we couldn't even talk to him. Occasionally I didn't want to visit him because I felt very dizzy and nauseous along the way. On days when we set off on the road to visit my father, I would not enter the last class but instead waited for my mother to pick me up in front of the school. When my mother came, we would take my brother and set off. We used to pray to my father and uncles there when we were on the road.

After all that happened, I almost lost control of my feelings. I would be nervous and angry, excited and happy at the same time.

I was very saddened by what I experienced on the last contact visit before the release of my father. What I experienced that day shook my nerves. My mother was going to come to school to pick us up, but she was a bit late. I began to think that they had gone to visit him without me. My mother finally showed up and we set out immediately, but we were 15 minutes late and we weren't allowed in. After waiting for so long and driving a long distance, not being able to see our father was devastating and I collapsed in front of the door and cried loudly. Fortunately, my father was set free at the court trial the next day. However, the reason he was released was a sad one. My grandfather had been diagnosed with cancer, due to the grief my father went through during this period the medical reports helped his partial and restricted freedom. We lost my grandfather three days after my father was released. There is much more to write, but I do not want to talk about it anymore. One day everything will be fine, I know and I look forward to it.

WE KEEP DREAMING

Written by: Berna, 12

"I look forward to my father's arrival. I grow in hope and trust in my Lord."

My name is Berna, I am 12 years old. I've been with good people since I was born. When I was two or three years old, I started covering my head with a hijab and went with my parents to iftar tents to help poor people. When I was of school age, we moved to another city and I had a very good school. When the director there wanted me to choose either a baby or a jersey, I chose a baby.

One evening, my father said that some uninvited guests might come to our house. I didn't quite understand who could be the uninvited guests? My father told us that it was not good for us to stay at home, and so we immediately prepared to leave.

It was almost evening, we said goodbye to the city

and set off on a long, dark road. It was our first trip without my father. On the way there the police stopped us. It was a simple traffic control, but my mother was white with fear, trembling. At the same time, she tried not to show her fear to us. Thankfully, we did not experience anything unfortunate. We set out on the road again, but this time we confused the road due to darkness. Then we saw the bus to our hometown in front of us so we started to follow it and eventually reached our destination.

My grandparents were very worried, and came out and waited for us at that late hour. When we got home, we took our luggage upstairs and told my grandmother and grandfather about our journey. We had dinner and went to bed. We stayed with my grandparents for a few months. My father had found another house for us and moved our belongings there. He gave my mother the good news, but he wanted to surprise us, so my mother did not tell us that my father had rented a new house and moved our things.

We got ready and my mom told us that our car had to stay here for a while and we were going to take the train to our new home. I was truly happy when she said we were going to get on the train, but at the same time I was very sad that we would abandon our car. This would be our first train trip. Our journey aboard the train finally started. We boarded the train in the evening and got off in the morning. Finally we reached our house. My mother said, "Let's wash our hands and face". While we were washing our hands and face, my mother called out, "Will you come out and take a look here". At that moment, I saw my father and I was very happy. After a short hug, he took us to our new home, which was a beautiful two-story house. Somehow, we settled in that house in a short time and of course I helped my mother. We had our first meal there in our room, and though it was our first day, everyone was able to sleep in their own bed.

After a while, we moved to another house. This house was not two-story, but it was beautiful. It was now time for me to start the 1st grade. How did I know that my separation adventure had begun? I was taken to my aunt's house. I had a hard time learning to read and write there, and cried almost every day. It was good for me to be able to talk to my parents, even for half an hour. Towards the end of the 1st grade, the school would be closed for a week or two and I would be reunited with my mother and father. In those days, we got a call from a friend of my father's. I was devastated when my aunt told me that my father had been detained. Before long, the police, who had taken my father into custody, came back to our house, turned the entire house upside down and took my brother and mother away.

That night I couldn't sleep for a long time, I saw my mother, father and brother in a dream. They were sitting on the ground side by side. I was standing and in front of me was a big, old, saucy policeman who acted like he was making fun of us. I was very angry, and shouting at the police, but the man was gawking at me. When I woke up, I couldn't get out of the dream. I was still fighting in bed. There was about one week left before the school closes; my teacher gave us a beautiful poem on Wednesday and said, "Memorize this." I memorized it on Thursday. I was the best performing student in school to recite this poem. This was my last day and my last achievement in that class.

We set off early on Friday. We went to my aunts because they had released my mother thankfully, with electronic handcuffs. I hugged my mother and sister. Then my mother put our best clothes on us as we were going to my father's place, but she couldn't come with us. When I saw my father, I realized how much I missed him. I wanted to cry, but I was held back from crying, because I sensed that if I cried, my father would cry too. Even so, my father had already started to cry. We went back and told my mother what had happened. Within a few months, my mother's electronic handcuffs were taken off and we stayed in our own house.

Sometimes we dream: When my father comes home

we will buy a caravan and take a tour of Turkey. When can we do it? I look forward to my father's arrival. I grow in hope and trust in my Lord.

TIME AND US

Written by: Nur

"Time cannot be undone. We do not know its beginning and the end. We cannot see the future, but we can adjust it..."

Back then, we were innocent children who had not yet met the dark side of the world. All we wanted was games, friends, fun. We were living the best life we could live, in a well-established order. Don't mind me saying it like that. At that time, even the most insignificant thing occupied a huge place in our eyes and hearts. I used to go cycling with my father on the weekends. I remember very well the day I started riding a bicycle. My father used to take us once a month to eat İskender kebab. Eating the kebab at this particular place was certainly different. Those days were our happiest days.

My primary school was an absolutely perfect place. At that time, I went to a private school because we were financially in very decent shape. I can say that this school and my teachers constituted the primary factors shaping my current character as well as my core values and behavior. In short, everything was as it should be back then. With our childish minds, everything was as good as it could get, until our lives changed abruptly, like being pushed off the edge of a cliff.

The date is July 15, 2016. I remember that night very well and the fear inside us. It reveals a shadow that lurks inside me, like a part of me. It pulls it out of the mists and brings it before my eyes. Fighter jets were flying low with sounds enough to deafen one's ears. The TV set was almost shaking from the vibrations of the jets' sonic waves. I went to my mother and she hugged me, stroked my hair. A fear fell on me at that moment, the reason for it I did not know, but I would soon understand . People were flocking outside. Those who fought, those who fled, those who ran, those who died… Did those who died there die for a just cause? Was flocking outside really the solution?

My mom used to tell me, "Whoever gets the most benefit out of something, they are its perpetrators." Then everything made more sense, but also became more deplorable.

I went to my grandparents that summer. I used to go every summer anyway, but that summer was different. One evening, the doorbell rang, and I called out, "Who is it?" My uncle came but I couldn't recognize him from the voice. Then my grandmother called out "who is it" and when she heard my uncle's voice and opened the door, she literally collapsed. My uncle was standing at the door with a backpack and suitcase. My grandmother hugged my uncle and cried. That day, for the first time, I saw an adult cry. My joy at my uncle's arrival suddenly gave way to mixed feelings. Why did my uncle come? Why is my grandmother crying? What happened? It turned out that they unfairly fired my uncle. He said "Instead of them comforting me, it was me who consoled them."

It was neither a beginning nor an end. It was just a vicious wheel of injustice that I could not understand at the time. Afterwards, some of our relatives were imprisoned. As we were getting ready to go to Middle School, the school was closed, so I was going to enroll in a new school. We were going to move to a new house. It was both exciting and sad, but there was nothing to be done. Our new house was fine, but our school... My grandmother used to say in the past jokingly whenever I went there, "I'll enroll you in that school so you stay with us permanently." How could I have known that one day that word would come true?

Now we had a completely different city, a completely different house, a completely different school and a completely different life. Nothing would ever be the same again. We were not fully aware of this, but a feeling inside us was thrusting this fact like a needle into our souls.

That was the first time I went to a public school. At first, I won't lie, I was scared of public schools. I dreamed of a place with bad boys, filthy toilets, and worn-out benches. In part they were all true, but then I realized it wasn't so bad after all. Eventually, we had to get used to it.

The students in our class were definitely different from me. Very different. Or should I say, I guess I was different from everyone else. Everyone dressed in a certain style, watched video games and YouTube channels that I didn't know about. At the age of 10, we either exist or we don't, but I felt that we were excluded. They were not like me, they spoke the same language and understood each other, but they wouldn't let me in. I finally met girls from the next class at the cooking club. We met and talked, and I felt that I warmed toward them.

I was told back then that contact visits are better than closed views because you can hug your father, whereas the closed views are through glass. Of course, I didn't understand anything. Until one evening in February of 2017, when the police came to the house, they broke in and searched everywhere, while all the children went into another room. We had no clue what was going on. I tried to hush my little brother, while trying to find out what was going on. At the same time, I was worried the cops would find my diary and read it. Yes, that's how young and naive I was. They took my father from work that day; he hasn't come back yet, but I hope he comes soon.

My grandmother was with us when we received my father's first letter. I read the letter, although I did not understand much, my brain was somehow aware of how serious everything was. When I finished reading the letter, I went and hugged my grandmother's neck, sobbing. Things didn't go well after that.

The first challenge was that everyone knew us there and so we couldn't stay anymore. My mother had been expelled from her job, which made it difficult for her to make a living there. We moved in with my grandmother. Of course, for a 2+1 house, it was fun at first, because going to my grandma's was great in itself.

Years followed each other after that. My father's trials were constantly postponed. After about 3.5-4 years, he was sentenced to nine years on trivial grounds. We were very hopeful that he would get out, but this didn't happen. Not much happened after that. I wrote poems and songs inspired by my experiences in this process. It's been years

Stories of Hope

now. It happened in our childhood.

In fact, doesn't maturity mean that a person has lived longer than necessary? People always appreciate the mature, but never ask about which ordeals did one attain this maturity.

You are not a child the moment you embrace the false world...

You are not a child the moment you start worrying about things beyond your homework...

You are not a child when you realize that colors are used as curtains to cover the gray.

You are not a child when you learn that an adult can cry too...

You are not a child the moment you see what is behind your experiences, the moment you hate, the moment you hold grudges...

Each soul is compelled to add faults on their timeline when they are tested. Time cannot be undone. We do not know the beginning and the end. We cannot see the future, but we can adjust it.

Whoever did this to us will not be able to bring back our lost years. Therefore, it is our duty to make up for the past in the future. Showing the truth to people, trying to prevent such things from happening again, learning from the past and improving ourselves as much as possible… That is our task. Every challenge has a purpose. The sole purpose of humanity is to understand the purpose of these tests and act accordingly.

BITTER AND SWEET MOMENTS

Written by: Melike

"May my Lord reward you in this world and in the Hereafter as much as infinite times the number of tears you wiped away."

It was a day in August five years ago. I had just received news that my favorite school was going to be shut down. I was very sad and cried. Teacher Hakan was our favorite teacher. No matter how heavy we were, when we hurt our feet, he would take us to the 4th floor to the hospital on his own lap. I have never seen such dedication in other teachers. The university my parents went to also closed and we were utterly broke. One morning the police came to take my mother away, but luckily we escaped them. I started to wake up from nightmares to check up on my mother.

I kept asking my mother, "When will all this pass?" Financial difficulties were nothing, but the prospect of my mom and dad going to jail terrified me.

During one day of Ramadan, my father was caught on the street and spent a week in a prison far from us. They called my mother, who went there on her own. I am very fond of my mother and father. I am a girl and I have always been treated like a baby-in-arms. Fortunately, they released her. I couldn't hold back my tears when I heard the news at school and cried a lot.

Five years have already passed and I had hoped it was over now, hoping everything would l be alright soon. My mother tried to hide it, but I could sense her fear every night that there would be a knock on the door. She wandered around the house at night and checked the door to see if anyone was coming.

Thank god my grandparents took care of our expenses. We tried to be happy as much as we could by taking the children of families like us to the movies, giving them cake and buying them clothes. My mother enjoyed it immensely and we did too. We understood that people are happy when they make others happy. When you live to make someone else happy, not just yourself, God makes you very happy as a gift. Of course, provided that you do it for the sake of Allah alone...

I hope these days will end one day! We pray for this. I want to go to Disneyland when we have money and when all these troubles are over. In fact, we have grown a lot in the face of all these tribulations and have become adults. God bless you for praying for us and rushing to our aid. May my Lord reward you in this world and in the Hereafter as much as infinite times the number of tears you wiped away.

THOSE WHO DESERVE PARADISE

Written by: Selma

"There is only one place worthy of them, and that is heaven, where they will be rewarded for enduring these tribulations."

I was very young when my mother's older brother went to prison; I didn't understand what was going on. My mother cried and everyone was sad. I still remember something my uncle's daughter told me when I was little: "When the police were taking my father away, my father said to me, 'I'll be back in three days,' but it has been three years and he still hasn't returned. It's been a long time, and I've grown up but now I understand what's going on."

Their situation was not easy at all and I felt very sorry for them. I prayed especially for my uncle after every daily ritual. One day my parents were going to visit my uncle and I wanted to go with them too, but they didn't take me.

Another day, my parents went to see him again, this time they took me. It would be a surprise to my uncle and I was so excited. When I saw my uncle, I couldn't help myself, I cried. I touched his hand through the glass. I was very upset, why was there glass between us? Why couldn't I hug him? But at the same time, I was very happy because I saw my uncle for the first time in a long time. While I was crying, my uncle's eyes also welled up with tears. I tried not to cry so that he wouldn't be upset.

I had friends, some of whom didn't have fathers and I felt very sorry for them, but I tried not to show it. I didn't use the word "dad" and I didn't talk much with my father when they were around so that they wouldn't be sad. I did all of this for my friends sake, because I had experienced that feeling too. What could we do for them? There were two things: one to pray and the other not to make them feel the absence of their father. That's why we were trying to spend more time with them. For instance we invited them on a picnic. My favorite part of all this was to see them happy. For example; they eagerly looked forward to the day of the picnic and after the day was over, they said it was their best day ever.

There was also an older sister, who we loved very much. She would listen to our troubles right to the end and would laugh even if what we said was not funny. In short, she would cry with us when we cried, and laugh with us when we laughed. She would take us to the theater, or a picnic, and meet us in the park. She invited us to her house and would read the Qur'an with us, and we would pray together and eat together.

Yes, so it's now time to talk about my family. I went to kindergarten at the school where my parents taught and it was beautiful. I still remember the interior. I wish I had studied first grade there, but the school closed. My mother and father were now unemployed. My father worked in a store after losing his job. Sometimes he whitewashed, sometimes he sold figs, he sold oil, but at the end of all of them, he said "the profession I do best is teaching". From the outside, my family seemed lucky. We were more fortunate than others, but I think this: My father and mother used to work as teachers abroad for a while and were separated from their families but they missed their country for years. Now I think that their current situation of not being separated from the ones they love might be a reward for the years of longing they had to endure abroad.

We are currently living in my grandmother's house. I think we are very lucky because some families could not take their children with them. They could not look after them, could not protect them and I feel very sorry for them. Unfortunately, even the grandmothers of some of my friends did not like them and did not want to see them. Thank God my grandparents are taking care of us. They love us and I love them too. Hopefully, we will move into our own house too.

God willing, the aunts and uncles in prison will regain their freedom and their broken families will be happy again. I have a dream that no one suffers, everyone goes on a picnic with their family, friends or relatives, and goes to the beach. I also dream of having fun with my own family, friends and relatives. I want a world where everyone loves each other, is tolerant towards each other, and does not know what prejudice is. People will try to help others without thinking about their own troubles, and those who patiently withstand these troubles, will be rewarded in paradise with abundant, much better and more beautiful provisions compared to what they lost in this world. I'm sure of that, because they deserve it, and so much more. There is only one place worthy of them, and that is heaven, where they will be rewarded for enduring these tribulations.

TEARS OF JOY

Written by: Defne

"...in that exact moment, even if you hug and kiss your father a hundred times, you cannot get enough. Because you think you will never see him again."

Hello, I'm Defne. When I was four years old, during my afternoon nap, there was a knock at the door. When my parents opened it, they saw the cops! The cops said what they had to say and took my father away. When I woke up, I looked for my father, but I could not find him. I looked in all the rooms five times, but he was not there. I asked my mother, "Where is my father?" My mother said, "Your daddy had an urgent job to attend to, he'll be back soon." I said, "OK."

Some time has passed, yet my father didn't return. I waited for days, he still didn't come and I cried. I cried… One day I drew a picture. In that picture, I drew my father falling into the sea, drowning and dying. When my mother saw my drawing, she could not stand it and took me to my father. I was very happy to finally see him. While I was talking to him as I wanted, the bell rang. The meaning of this bell is "time's up, it's time to leave". The bell had a very, very bad sound. Iyyy! It's time to part now. I started crying and I was sad. In other words, if you are in that situation, even if you hug and kiss your father a hundred times, you cannot get enough, because you think you will never see him again.

I cried a lot when I got home; a lot. That's how time passed, and passed, and passed... Why do you think I came to this point after thinking about all these things? I spent four birthdays without a father. I have uncles, aunts, older sisters, grandmothers, and mother. There are gifts, there is cake, there is a candle, but something is missing. The most important detail... The most indispensable thing... My father... Think about it; how very painful it was to go through what I just told you about four times, while my father spent four years in prison, all in vain. My father and the innocent people inside are wrongly being tried and people do not know about these events.

What if the situation were reversed? My father is with me, but my mother is not? This would be even much worse. Or, if they took mom and dad at the same time. This would definitely be much worse. In other words, I would be like an orphan. Orphans are children whose parents have died, but neither my mother nor my father died. My father was finally released, but there are still many kids whose fathers are in prison.

When I went to the prison, I didn't like the bars

at all. When I had to leave my father, I felt nauseous, uncomfortable, and cried incessantly. Sometimes we talked from behind bars, and the iron railings were covered with glass. We weren't able to open the iron bars anyway, so what was the point of glass? That's the closed view I'm talking about. The ominous bell during the contact visit, turning off the lights suddenly during the closed view, and the door-locking… Those were all awful and I felt imprisoned there too, with nowhere to run to or escape. One evening while I was with my father , I sang to him with my guitar and recorded it.

One day my mother and I went to give new clothes to my father. They held my mom and me there for a while. They were going to keep her in remand prison for a day and I was going to stay with my aunt. That day I realized that even a night without my mother would be scary and as despairing as the apocalypse.

My father was released on the day when my mother had to stand trial. My mother and other friends went to court and after a couple of hours, she returned and told me to get ready soon. She said my uncles were setting off to get my father. "Is my father out?" I asked. My mother said, "Not only your father, but also other fathers came out." We went and waited for my father for about an hour in front of the prison. After some time, the door of the prison opened and fathers started to walk out. It took some time beforeI could see my father and I cried while I waited for him. Before all of this I didn't know people could shed tears of joy but for the first time, I knew it was possible.

PRAY FOR GOOD DAYS

Written by: Serhat, 9

"Or did terrorist mean good criminal? Teachers were guilty of teaching people goodness and righteousness. So weren't those who accused them good and righteous people?"

Let me introduce myself. My name is Serhal Can, I am nine years old and I'm in 3rd grade.

My mother and father said that my sister would start first grade and they would enroll me in kindergarten. When my sister went to kindergarten, she had very nice coloring books, pencils, crayons and pastels. When I go to kindergarten, I would also have coloring books and paints just like my sister. I was going to play and have fun with my friends there,so I was very happy to go to kindergarten.

While I was in the village for a summer vacation, my father told me that the school my sister and I were going to was closed. My father was now unemployed. The police came to search the houses of his friends and teachers at the school where he had worked. That's why we stayed in the village. One day, my father came to the village and said to my mother, "the police came and searched the house, wrote a report and left." Then a short time before the opening of the schools, we returned to our home. However, before long, the police started looking for my father and summoned him to the court. My father's friends and teachers were arrested. Some of them were the fathers of my friends. My friends and their families were upset that they were left without a father. We were all sad and surprised, but there were some children who had both parents arrested, not only their father but also their mother, and they were much more upset.

Meanwhile, when my father became unemployed, he started looking for a job. My father was actually a teacher, but he was now working as a porter. Like my father, unemployed teachers were also working in other jobs. I saw many uncles and aunts who used to be teachers selling different things in the bazaar. At the time, I didn't know exactly what "terrorist" meant. But it confused me that these good people, most of whom were teachers, were called terrorists. Or did terrorist mean good criminal? Teachers were guilty of teaching people goodness and righteousness. So were those who accused them not good and righteous people?

My father was trying to buy and sell olive oil, figs, apricots and honey. He brought home sacks of figs and apricots. My mother and father chose the good ones, and then my sister and I would weigh and package them. My father sold the good ones, and we ate the others. My sister started school then. She was not going to the beautiful school of her dreams, but to a distant place with packed classrooms. My sister used to go with my father early in the morning every day, and they returned together in the evening. My sister's school ended in the afternoon, but she had to wait for my father until the evening. That's how the semester ended.

One day, while my mother and I went to the hospital, the police came to our house and asked the man on the top floor where my father worked. They cautioned him not to tell us anything about their visit. Why did they want to hide their visit? What did they want from my father and what would they do? My father was already working out of town. He didn't come home most of the time. One evening, the police came in two cars, and asked where my father was. My mother said she didn't know. They wanted to search the house. My mother asked about the search warrant. "We don't have a search warrant," said the cops.

Someone waited in front of the house and they came back an hour later with a search warrant. They searched for my father at home. Unaware of anything happening around us, my sister and I were showing the pictures we made and our toys to the police. They had come to take my father from us. There were people who accused my father of crimes and the police were after him.

My mother, sister and I went to my mother's village after these events. My sister started going to school in the village. Gendarmes came to the village to look for my father. Seven or eight soldiers with rifles in their hands surrounded the village house and searched it. They asked my mother where my father was. "We haven't seen each other for long, I don't know where he is now," she said. My mother was also frightened, thinking they were coming to get her. So my mother and I left the village a few days later. My sister was left alone with my grandmothers in the village, to go to school. We were very sad when we left her there. Our family was shattered. My father is somewhere, my sister is somewhere, my mother and I are somewhere else. We all parted unintentionally. A few months later, when the schools closed, my father rented a one-room place for us to be together, but we didn't stay long there either. Unfortunately, they found us there and arrested my father. Now I learned what prison was. Happiness is far from us now. My mother always says good days will come and says let's pray. I pray for good days to come, too.

PAST AND FUTURE

Written by: Zeynep, 15

"...I will study law and do my best to bring justice to this country where there is no justice."

I'm Zeynep, I'm in 10th grade. My purpose in writing this is to share my perspective about the difficulties that people like us go through. When I was 10, they came to our house at 7 in the morning one day and took my father away. He was taken by his fellow police officers with whom he had worked in the past. His colleagues had handcuffed him. I cried so much that the people in the building woke up and came to our house. I actually didn't understand what was going on. I cried because everyone was crying. My best friends ostracized me because my father was arrested, and they cornered me and beat me. It may sound like some insignificant matter while reading this, but in reality it was a very agonizing experience for me.

After my father was arrested, his family told us to leave our house. As if we didn't have enough problems, we now had to deal with my father's family. The thing that aggrieved me the most in these difficult times was that our relatives acted with the same malice that others did to us. Anyway, we went to the prison on our first visit. Everyone was crying and it was very crowded. There were many prohibitions and rules. My father was grief-stricken. At the end of our meeting his cheeks were smiling, but his heart was broken and filled with pain. During our first contact visit, there was a fight at our table while everyone was catching up with each other. My grandparents didn't let my mom continue using our car so we had to give it to my uncle, and we moved to a house in another city.

My father was in one city and we were in another. We used to see my father's face once every two months. I just passed 5th grade. On the first day of school, my mother went to visit my father and we had to stay at our grandmother's. We didn't have a home then. That's why I suffered a lot. April 7 was my birthday, the first birthday without my dad. I was not in a good mood. In the music class, my mother, sister and two aunts entered the classroom with a birthday cake. Actually, I wasn't happy at all, but I pretended to be enjoying the moment to make them happy. In the evening, I cried silently when I went to bed, because my mother was also crying at night when we slept. This is how my first fatherless birthday went.

My father was later sentenced to 6 years and 3

months in prison. I started a school after being forced to enroll in one. No one knew that my father was in prison in that school, because even the teachers were shouting, "There are still a lot of 'FETO' members everywhere," and swearing at innocent people like my father. I couldn't tell anyone about my problem and nor could I cry. I got shingles from depression. For two weeks I couldn't sleep at night because of the pain, I had eczema and numbness in my hands. It happens again when I still push myself or get upset. For two years, we went to another city to visit my father. The visit was at 8 am, so we were on our way at around 2:30-3:00 in the morning. Finally, my father was transferred to the city we were in. My mother went to visit him every week. Two years passed like this and my father came to us in April 2020. The gendarmes left him in the coach station. He didn't have a phone and didn't know where our house was. He was left with bags in his hands. My father had a childhood friend whose house was nearby, so he went to him and the friend brought him to us.

It can snow in the city where we lived, even in April, and the house was very old, had only one stove in one room, and the doors and windows were in tatters. It didn't catch the sun and it didn't get warm at all. Everytime my mother came from the kitchen, she would sit by the stove trying to warm up. The windows in our room were broken, when you closed them, they wouldn't open and if you could open them, they wouldn't close again. We lived in such a house for four years and everyone kept telling us "You get to be satisfied and thankful for what you have." When my father was released and finally saw our house, he said, "You can't live in this house, how could you live in this house for four years?" We moved in June.

My father used to be a policeman and now he sells tahini in the markets. A prison guard asked me one day, "What do you want to be when you grow up?" When I answered him, "I will be a lawyer to make people like you pay for what you have done to us and get revenge for all others like us", even the guard's eyes filled with tears. I am currently a heart patient; I have a leaky heart valve. I am 15 years old. I will ask for an account for every drop that falls from the eyes of children like me, innocents like my father, and those who cry like my mother and sister. I will study law and I will do my best to bring justice to this country where there is no justice. I will not give my rights to those who did this evil to us and those who supported them, both in this world and in the Hereafter. Finally, I reunited with my father, but dozens of children are separated from their parents. May Allah make them reunite with their families soon. I wanted to be the voice of everyone. I hope I have been one.

Stories of Hope

BRAVERY

Written by: Seyma

"The good always lose because the good always fight fair"

I got up in the morning to go to school. Then I saw the cops at the door. I couldn't understand what was happening. They went in and searched the house. The house was turned into a battlefield. They took my father away from our house in handcuffs. In that moment, I learned what helplessness means. Three days later, in the evening, my mother and I went to the courthouse. Everyone there was crying and shouting. Then they arrested my father. The moment I saw his face behind bars, I cried too. Four days later, the police took my mother as well. Then I really understood everything more clearly. Everyone was crying.

Four days later, we were in the prison where my father was being kept for the first visit. My mother wasn't with us since she also had her court hearing. We went through a search, X-rays, guards, eye scans, authentications and more... I wanted to go inside and see my father as soon as possible. Long rows of tables... They made me meet with my father in a dark place. We hugged each other and cried. It saddened me to see him there in that closed space. It was so sad to see the sorrow and despair in my father's eyes after he learned that my mother had been in court and might be arrested. The meeting ended in 45 minutes. Then we started to wait for my mother in front of the courthouse. She would either be arrested or come to us. This one hour was no different from the silence of death. Then came the good news. My mother was released. Indeed, I realized when I met my mother that there were no handcuffs for hope.

A year later, my brother managed to win a science high school and my elder sister was able to enroll in a medical school. I was in the third grade. We were holding on to life somehow. Our successes were actually a lesson to everyone and a proof that we were standing straight in the face of the baptism of fire. The transfer of my father to a more distant prison had dealt a harsh blow to us all, but I remained standing. Because if you've hit rock bottom, the only place you're going is up. After a year, my sister was studying medicine and my brother was attending science high school. I was in the 4th grade. We could not always go visit my father, because the round trip took two days. We all had school. Four years later, my father was still in prison. During this time, I passed the scholarship exam.

In this process, everyone turned their back on us and we were ostracized from society. But this did not deter us. We have continued our success and will continue to do so. Actually, I think the world is in its current condition because we are not as brave as the bad guys. My experience shows that "The good always lose, because the good always fight fair."

NORMAL COURSE OF EVENTS

Written by: Beyza, 18

"...it is necessary to continue living without being frozen in time, to love life no matter what."

These events started in the year I was preparing for the university exam. My father kept exhorting us to give particular importance to our education and get a good job, and always advised us "don't neglect your studies" amidst all the turbulence in our lives. One morning, the police came, I was not very nervous as it was something I was waiting for. They searched the house and took my father. Three days later my father was arrested. At that time, I was not devastated, as I could not have predicted that five years would pass without my father. I thought it would only be a few months. Four days after my father was arrested, the cops came for my mother. This time I was not as cold-blooded as I had been when they came for my father. It was one of those moments when I felt the most helpless. They were going to take my mother away soon, and there was nothing I could do. I was very afraid and could not have imagined that she would be arrested.

I watched the police take my mother away on the news channels. There was nothing that I could do. It was one of the hardest days of my life. The trial day came and thankfully they released her. I was relieved, but I couldn't shrug off the great fear that she would be taken again.

Since then, I have always been anxious. It was as if life had stopped for me. I thought everything would be alright, so I could move on with my life. I felt frozen at one point in time and became depressed. Everyone's life was normal. We were experiencing things we couldn't even imagine. I was isolated from the world. For someone who attached great importance to the university exam, experiencing these events increased my exam stress even more. Then I thought to myself. that I would recover soon. Even if these troubles continued unabated like this, they mustn't be allowed to snatch anything away from me. I promised myself to continue to improve, reconnect with life and love life again. No matter what, I would not give up on life. I was going to be a little selfish and look at my own life.

Thank goodness I passed the exam. I got my dream medical school with a good degree. Looking back over the past five years, I'm glad I didn't give up. And most importantly, I realized this: There is no such thing as a 'normal course' in life. My approach was never right, as if my father would come and everything would go back to normal, I would put my life in order once these events were over. Unexpected things happen in everyone's life. It is necessary to accept that this is the normality of life, to continue living without being frozen in time, to love life no matter what. Five years hasn't taken anything away from me. Yes, they passed away without my father, but they have given me so much. If I looked at everything as ruined, if I had left life, five years would still pass the same. My father would not come again, but I would not be able to add anything to myself, I would not have been able to realize my dreams and, in short, I would have been defeated.

I hope these days will pass and I am very sure that they will pass. I strongly believe that, even if he intentionally delays sometimes, Allah sooner or later brings out what is right and brings it out in the most beautiful way.

FATHERS AND THEIR JOBS

Written by: Zumra, 7

"I hope all distant workplaces will be closed."

My name is Zumra. I am seven years old. I am going in to 2nd grade. My father went off to work in a distant place when I was two years old. He had to work there for 10 years. My father works at K. I go there to see him on Fridays, and we talkon the phone. My mother also talks to him. I wave to him as I leave,and my mom waves her hands too. I read him the poems I learned at school.

He asked me to share the poems I learned with him and so I recited the poem "my father". He was very happy. I also sang the National Anthem. "Well done girl," he said. My father writes me beautiful letters, and I also write to him. I tell him "to come back to our house", but he says the angry, bad manager wouldn't allow him to leave. My father wanted to come to our house, but he couldn't. He was teaching people who had bad behavior at work. My father is a very happy person; he always makes me laugh. I only see him during recess at noon and I wish I could have seen him longer!

I can't sit next to him because of the coronavirus. I don't like talking on the phone. I want my father to come to our house and drop me off at school. My mother doesn't drive very well. When my father comes, I want to play with him, go to the basketball, go to the park, paint and go on vacation. I want to sleep with him at night.

I don't tell anyone about my father's workplace. My mother says to me, "Daughter, this is our secret." I ask "Daddy, how many days do you have to work?" He says "My job can take too long, daughter." I can't even wait 100 days. I feel very sorry when he says that, but I have to wait a lot. He buys me gifts with the money he earns at work. I love my father. When I go to bed, I read my sleep prayer and say, "O God, bring our father to our house, amen". Let everyone's father come home! I hope that distant workplaces will be closed!

HAPPY ENDING

Written by: Sena, 18

We are always missing a part of ourselves and our minds are always with people who are in the same situation as us. I hope one day we can write a happy ending to this story.

I'm Sena, and I am 18 years old. My father has been in prison for four years. To my father, I am still 14 years old. The last time my life was still normal, was the day when this strange adventure started; I was 14 years old.

One morning during a day when we were staying at my grandmother's house in the village, we woke up to the sound of the phone. The neighbor called my father saying "the police came for you". Of course, we were waiting like everyone else back then, but we were still shocked when it happened. The police called the house looking for my father and also summoned my mother for a statement. My mother was suspected of having cancer at the time, so there was no way that she could go to prison. So there was actually a bigger reason besides her innocence. When she returned from the village, my mother did not stay in our house again. I don't know how many months have passed like this.

While all this was going on, I was going to the 8th grade, it was my exam year. But my biggest concern was unfortunately not the exam. So months passed and my exam day came. Since my school is close to home, my father and I would stay at home. We were going to pick up my mother and brother from where they were staying and go to my exam place. What a reasonable plan when you put it that way. That morning my father woke me up and said, "Sena, the cops are here. My daughter, get dressed and go to the exam by yourself, and I will come later after giving a statement." 'I will come.' I didn't believe that sentence then either, but I didn't expect it to take this long either. The cops searched the whole house. Although they found nothing, they took my father and left. Neither my mother nor anyone else knew. It's still not clear at all.

I remember that I couldn't even react because I had to prepare immediately and take the exam. Anyway, I walked to the exam. I got two mistakes from that TEOG. I think those two wrong answers are the least of what those people owe me. The funny thing is that my father was a teacher that day, so there was an exam task. He was in prison the evening of the day he was preparing to become an exam invigilator. Like hundreds of thousands of people... Who had what plan? They were convicted for a crime they didn't commit. In those days, we were sad about them, because we were unaware that we would be sad for four years. We were unaware that what we would lose would be not only that day, but four whole years of our lives. Birthdays, graduations, anniversaries, successes, failures... We didn't realize they would all be gone.

If I continue... My father was detained for 13 days and my mother was not able to visit at that time because she was a 'fugitive'. I provided the dialogue between my mother and father, and I provided what my father needed. It went on like this for months after he was imprisoned. The visiting room, which the 15-year-old me and my eight-year-old brother shared with many people who had the same pain only in different forms... But one day, after a visit on a religious feast day, my mother's family learned about our situation. They would not have been able to digest this either, they said, "How can our daughter live hiding, like a fugitive?" They came and took us back. For what? To turn my mother over to the police and clear her. A day or two later, my mother went to the police with my uncle, her own brother. The reason for this was that my uncle thought he could help, even though my mother might never have come back from there. But luckily she came back three days later and had the cyst removed from her breast, which I referred to as suspected cancer.

Then our new normal was to live in this new city we were taken to overnight. We lived there for a year. While my father was in prison in another city, my mother would go to see him either once a month or once every two months. A year passed in this way and we are back. Last year while we were living our messed up lives as normal, my mother was suddenly arrested. She was summoned for an interrogation and the lawyer assured her saying "nothing will happen". For the second time, I heard the promise of 'I will return', which would again last longer than I thought. I prepared a suitcase for my mother. My grandfather and grandmother were also staying with us and we went to the contact visit together. It was so strange

Stories of Hope

to see my mother there. After visiting my father, my mother and I used to walk out of the prison together and comfort each other. But now that my mother was behind bars, after visiting her and leaving the prison, I had no one to console and no one was there to console me either. I had a brother, whom I tried every day to make believe that my mother would come home right away... what I was most concerned about for the past two months... Because I didn't want him to go through all this at the age of eleven. No children should have to. None of us should have had to. And none of us deserved to have so many years stolen from our lives.

How many weeks passed, at school, in class, waiting for a phone call from my mother. It was always during the classes that I learned that my mother had been transferred to another city and the result of her trial. While preparing for the university exam, I spent my time thinking about either my mother or my brother in the lessons that I had to listen carefully to. My mother got out of prison, but her mind remained with the people there. We can't fully cherish any joy in this period. We are always missing a part of ourselves and our minds are always with people who are in the same situation as us. I hope one day we can write a happy ending to this story.

UNDERSTANDING PEOPLE

Written by: Seda Nur

I hope our sisters and brothers get out of jail and get back to work. I hope the world becomes livable.

Hello, my name is Sena Nur. I live in the city of [A] with my mother, father and siblings. Now, don't feel sorry for us for what I'm about to tell you. We have never been enmeshed in a wretched state nor have we felt miserable. We lived in the city of [G] and my mother was appointed to civil service there. My father had bought a house there and had agreed to work as a teacher in a private school. Until July 15, things were perfect. Would you believe that, it was the first time I heard the word 'coup'. Hundreds of schools were closed, including the school I attended and the private teaching institution where my father worked. Frankly, I was in shock. They imprisoned benevolent and beautiful people who only wanted to teach people good things.

Most people were cut off from their families overnight, and many had to embrace an excruciating test that day. My mother and father are among those who lost their jobs and were estranged from their families. My mother was suspended from her job at the civil service. We went to my grandparents on vacation with my aunts and siblings.

Stories of Hope

Then my mother came, but I felt something strange. Our house was moving! I really couldn't understand that, until my aunts told me...

The police came to our house and searched the house, accusing my mother of being a terrorist. My mother was detained within a day and a half. My youngest brother was not even a year old, but we were left without a mother. Shortly after that my mother arrived, going to the police station twice a week and signing to prove that she was in that city. In this country, those who took a murderer into custody and yet released them without question were officially torturing innocent people, putting them in jail and wearing them out with lawsuits. This country is weird.

Schools opened. We only covered 15th of July for a week in schools! It's really unbelievable. With the opening of schools, expenses soared and financial difficulties began. My mother could not work anywhere. No one was hiring my father because of his record. My father finally got a job at a coffee shop. He used to leave around 6-7 in the morning and return home at 12 at night. The money he earned was nothing close to enough given our conditions at that time. He could not get a fair match for his labor at all. School expenses were somehow settled.

That year, my uncle, whom I called our supporter

and had said he would never betray us, complained that my parents were terrorists. My mother's case was ongoing and constantly being postponed. Summer has come and passed and schools have opened, along with the recurring expenses. My dad got a job at a course center and that was really great news. The financial conditions improved a little bit, yet we couldn't buy everything we needed. Still, we could be counted as much better off compared to before. Now I was in the 6th grade and I understood everything better. My mother's cases were still pending and thankfully were being postponed. I didn't know what we would do if my mother went to jail. My father was sued that year, for working in private teaching institutions and trying to teach people science and religion. A friend of his that he trusted the most, who ate and drank with him, became a 'confessor' and this caused my father to be sentenced to six years. My father's case is still pending and if the court approves, he will go to prison and we will be without a father.

I don't understand how a person's conscience can allow this to happen to an innocent person. That year, my uncle came to my father's workplace and shouted things like "You are a terrorist, you deserve to crawl in misery" to my father in a way that does not befit a human being. Huh... How weird are people?

Stories of Hope

The summer is over, my mom's cases are adjourned, and my dad's court case hasn't changed. Schools opened. Fortunately, my father agreed with two prep schools and started to receive enough salary to run the house. My siblings and I were going to school, and my father was going to his courses. My grandmother and grandfather used to protect and support us, and they still do. I really love them. One day that year, my mother had a court case. I came home, but the result was still not announced. We continued to wait in suspense, until my mother suddenly cried happily from inside and said, 'I have been acquitted'. Believe me, I have never experienced the lightness I felt at that moment anywhere else. Since my father went to give private lessons that day, he did not learn this until later..

That year I met an older sister who was in a similar situation like ours. My father introduced us and this older sister was really sweet, perfect and kind. How can I say it, she really made people want to smile. She has a son, and her husband got out of jail a week ago. I am really happy with this news.

I'm in the last year of middle school, the expenses have increased even more. I was happy that my mother's case was closed, but I was never quite at ease as my father's case was still pending. I took the high school exam and so the summer began. At least I got rid of exam stress during the summer. Then we couldn't go to school for a long time because of the coronavirus. This situation was bad for our lessons, for our finances and for our morale… Schools opened after a while and I started high school.

I started working with my father to help people like us this year. My father said we did this in order to extend a helping hand to our sisters and brothers in need. We went to a few people's homes and my father visited them and said, "Do you need anything?" Earlier, we had also visited houses to give sacrificial meat. Receiving the blessings of those people, making them happy and seeing them happy all the time was like therapy for me. I wish all these people could be happy one day and never have experienced such things. I went in to the 2nd year of high school, that is, the 10th grade. We moved to the village with my family, due to the pandemic and financial reasons. My family bought a few cows and they started to earn money by selling their milk to make a living. How can people stay so comfortable all these years while our older sisters and brothers are rotting in prison, doing all kinds of jobs except teaching, which is considered a sacred profession? It's hard to understand people!

Now we live in the village and we are still waiting for the verdict of my father's court case. I hope the prison sentence is not finalized and my father will not leave us.

Stories of Hope

Otherwise, my mother and all of us may stumble and fall, we don't know how long we can last. I hope everything will be alright one day. I hope our sisters and brothers get out of jail and get back to work. I hope the world becomes livable, that's all I ask. Stay well.

UNKNOWNS

Written by: Nur, 17

My pen is not enough to describe all that has happened. Maybe I just don't have the courage…

It all started the night of July 15… Who knew my life would turn upside down like this? Who could have said that all this would happen to me? Maybe I wouldn't believe it even if they told me. In the first years, I lived my life as if I was unaware of everything, but deep inside I knew something was wrong. My mother and father were always nervous; the house was always restless… This situation continued for a while, until my mom got fired. It was a difficult time for my mother and for us.

It was also a time when we were struggling financially. We had to move, and my school had also changed. It was very difficult for me to adapt to the new environment. I couldn't get used to it. I always felt so alone. For a long time, my life continued in a monotonous state. Everything seemed fine, but at the same time it wasn't. While the seasons were chasing each other like this, on a winter morning while I was still awake, the doorbell rang. I could more or less predict what might happen. Fear gripped me. I was thinking what if the police were at the door now. I left my room. My siblings were asleep, while my parents were in the hallway looking at each other with frightened and confused eyes. I felt so many emotions at once.

Yes, there were cops at the door and they were going to take my father away. I knew it!

While my mother went to open the door for the cops, I went into my room. I closed my door and buried my head in my pillow and started to sob. No one would hear my voice, or witness my sobs. I don't know how long I just stood there. My eyes were bloodshot. After a while, my mother came into the room. "Get ready, the cops are going to ask you a few questions," she said. I went to them and they asked me a few questions. I answered them all in a tired voice. The environment was very strange for me. The feeling of being in that room was awful, because I knew what would happen next. I knew why the cops were at my house. I thought of my father, and wondered how he was feeling now, or what he was thinking? The policeman in front of me was writing with his pen while

Stories of Hope

I was talking. Every time I heard the sound of the pen moving; the sound of it touching the paper, something inside me would break. I couldn't look into my father's eyes. I didn't dare, I was afraid of crying and upsetting him even more. What I felt and experienced during those minutes was terrifying.

The worst part was when we said goodbye to my father. I hugged him tightly, as if I never wanted to let him go, and we said goodbye, hoping there would not be a long separation. I didn't know where they were taking him, how they would treat him, or how he felt... I was trapped in a huge obscurity. I had to grapple with these feelings when I was only 13 years old. At 13, I had to get used to these grim experiences, and accept my father's absence.

After my father left, I didn't come to my senses for a long time. It took me a long time to accept them. I often thought of death. I thought it would all be over if I died, because I was crushed under the weight of what had happened. Death seemed to me the only escape route. My feelings also distanced me from people. I was always alone. I didn't want to talk to anyone. Words would cause new black holes to open in my mind. That's why I kept silent, afraid to even talk to myself. After my mother started noticing all this, she decided to take me to a psychologist.

I had a long period of psychological treatment, but my experiences left traces in my mind as a trauma, and they have not passed.

I know I will never forget what I went through. I am 17 years old now. I am a girl who has had to adjust to her new life. A girl struggling to not accept the life she's in. I have revealed to you a very small slice of my life. Maybe I just wanted to touch your heart, even a little. My pen is not enough to describe all that has happened, or maybe I just don't have the courage…

THE LAST CHOCOLATE

Written by: Fatmanur, 14

I wish I had my father by my side and not live in need of others.

After July 15, I felt that my life had changed completely. I was only nine years old, and I couldn't understand many things at that time, but I sensed that something was not right. Later I began to understand some of the things and that they were very serious. Too serious not to see my father for four years…

Gradually things were getting more serious. We were running because of something we hadn't done. I realized how serious it was when we moved, because my father was wanted for something he didn't do. I kept questioning this myself, "what did my father do?" That was the main thing that bothered me the most. My father was a member of a terrorist organization and of course this subject started to be talked about in schools. Everyone blamed the same thing and the same people. While they talked about it, it was impossible not to see the hatred in his eyes.

It was an ordinary day. I was punished for speaking during the class that day and had to buy chocolates for the whole class. I explained this to my father and he was very calm. He went out and got the chocolates and I greeted my father at the door, hugged him and thanked him. I slept happily at the thought of having chocolate tomorrow.

It was early morning the next day. My sister woke me up, crying. I couldn't grasp what was happening at first. "What happened?" I asked my sister. "The cops are here," she said. I didn't believe it at first, I remember asking her 2-3 times. When they arrived, I remembered starting to cry and going into the living room. I think my father was signing a few things and the cops were giving him orders. I remember him walking out of the door and the chocolates were there next to the door. My mother and sister were crying and I was crying too. I remember going to school that day, I taking the chocolate box with me and handing them out to my friends. I felt strange distributing them. The last thing my father bought me before he left was chocolate. I guess that's why I remember it.

Later there were trials, but my father could not come home. In every court, they said "this time he will be released," but for my father, this didn't happen. He was sentenced and imprisoned. Then the visits started and I saw a lot of people in the same situation as we were. The more I saw, the more my hatred towards certain people and things grew. I began hearing some stories of people in dire straits financially, and people with mental disorders... These were affecting me a lot. I eagerly awaited the contact visits where I would see my father and hug him, which was very strange to me.

The days passed somehow. Sometimes I really felt the absence of my father. There were court hearings, where hope is wished for every time, but always with negative results. Eventually the the final trial happened; my father was sentenced to prison, and I felt that I was getting used to my father's absence. Though I felt his absence sometimes… My high school entrance exam process started, and it was a very tiring, taxing period for me. During this period, I started to have panic attacks due to stress; my heart would start to pound where I stood, and that led me to see a psychiatrist. As the exam approached, my stress started to increase.

It was a difficult and fatherless period for me. At that time, my mother was also detained. In addition to the absence of my father, the separation of my mother also affected us seriously. I fell back on my studies during this period, I couldn't study, because I had tons of questions in my head; I wondered if my mother would come back; how long would she have to stay there? Then my mother came! Thank God she came, otherwise, I thought life would be very strange and awkward without either my father or my mother. Even though my mother's court process is still going on, I am happy that she is with us. I wish I had my father by my side and not have to live in need of others.

My father has two more years to serve. I hope this process ends as soon as possible and all these innocent people can return to their jobs and homes.

DESPAIR

Written by: Busra, 17

I still have high hopes that our lives that changed in one day will change once more in one day.

If the person I am today told the person I was in the morning of July 15, 2016, about the incredible events that she would experience and the strange situations she would fall into in the years ahead, then the me 6 years ago would most likely find all of it an incredibly bad joke. Troubles, too ominous even to be a bad joke, were about to become her fate and the fate of thousands of innocent people who were unaware of the great challenges that awaited them. We were about to face some truths that seemed impossible at the time. The morning of July 15, 2016 was not much different from other mornings. It was an ordinary day of any holiday until the evening hours. Of course, this ordinary course of events included my father, a police officer who was always on duty and who never had the opportunity to attend family holiday meetings. That is why he was not with us that evening, but in the city where we live.

The first time we saw what broke up the ordinary day was a banner of flash news flowing on the screen of the TV, and all the channels halted what they were streaming and went live. Violent images, massacred soldiers, so-called victory demonstrations are engraved in the minds of everyone who came after them… There was only one question in our minds, "what happened?" and after that "what will happen?" At least for that evening, it was somewhat comfortable, because my father was not working that day, and we had spoken on the phone. We believed he was safe. We were unaware that the days of real insecurity and fear had begun for us on that very day. My father would be with us in a few days to spend the last days of his vacation and then we would return home together. I didn't realize until my father came that all the arrows ready to fire after that night were aimed at us and the lives of thousands of innocent people like us. My father came and I saw in his face something bad was happening. My father came, all his joy replaced with an uneasiness, the source of which I did not know. He walked around the house with a mind that could be seen from afar, full of too many questions. It was as if there was a black cloud above his head.

His concern was not only for himself, but also for his wife, his three children, one of whom was three months old, and countless innocent companions. He was expelled. This was the first of the terms, the meaning of which I still can't grasp fully even today, but that I would have to learn in the process. We came back from that vacation in a strange confusion of mind. We came home. We didn't know what to do. We tried to continue our routines as much as possible. My father must have felt that these were the last days he could spend freely for a long time to come, he began to spend his days with his children.

We could no longer enjoy living, eating and drinking as before. As we saw what was going on around us and when all kinds of slanders and endless disasters began to rain down on people who were so docile as not to hurt even an ant deliberately, it became impossible to enjoy life. Every minute we heard that someone was suspended and that an investigation was launched against them. Things were not so bright for our own family. I had a brother at home who was born with adverse health conditions, had to undergo regular hospital screenings and was still a baby. This was perhaps the most worrying part of what happened to us. The fact that he had to be treated outside the province once a month brought along many new concerns. Moreover, all this happened in a very short time.

A few days before August, the police came to the house. My father and brother were out for a walk. The doorbell rang, when. I opened the door, I saw them; A group of policemen, the number of which I do not remember...My father's face, a chilling complexion mixed with sadness... They entered the house and started searching. What were they looking for? Even today I don't understand. It was something between making a search and turning the house into a battlefield. I remember a hum inside my head and the rest is blurry. When my father took the last money out of his pocket and gave it to my mother, I was sure that it was an unnecessary gesture. After all, my father would return in a few days at most. In fact, they took my father, not for a few days, but for many hundred days to come. The detention process is always somewhat full of hope. We want to hope that the people we love will come back. My father did not return for a long time. The three-day detention period was replaced by a two-year detention period.

I remember our first meeting like it was yesterday. The discomfort of having to come face-to-face with a torrent of adversities in the last few weeks, great anxieties about the uncertain future, the pain in my heart to see my father there, the bullying of the guards when I brought my brother, who is just over three months old, to the visiting place, and the unnecessary hardships that were deliberately created... I have a list. If I had to sum it up in one word, I would say "desperation".

It had been a week or so since my father was arrested.

Unfortunately, the doorbell rang again early one morning. Now I understand better how I got the paranoid feeling that developed in me against the knock on the door. A knock on the door sounds like a distress signal to me even today. This time the police had come to pick up my mother. Our house, which was searched for a short time ago, was searched thoroughly once again for some reason. A female police officer approached my library and took a book on Ottoman history. "This is a banned publication," she said. "But this is a book about Ottoman history," I said. "This broadcast was banned yesterday morning," she said. That day I learned that a book on Ottoman history could be "evidence for membership in a terrorist organization". They took bags of books from home along with my mother.

My brother was not yet weaned and so my mother wanted to take him with her. They said they couldn't allow this. They said to me, "You can bring him later to the station when your brother wakes up. If you can get permission, your mother will feed him, and you will take him back when she is finished feeding." Just as my father left the last money in his pocket, my mother advised me before leaving the house what formula I should use to feed my brother if she could not return in time. My mother left. The door was closed. My brother, who had been sleeping until then, woke up crying from his sleep. I myself was still a child. I was 14 years old. I didn't know what to do in the event of a possible 'mother absence'. I couldn't think of a relative or acquaintance I could turn to for support. The acquaintances I could go to were too old and far away to care for the baby. I said to myself, "We have good neighbors. If I can't do it, I'll ask for their help."

It was hard, but my subconscious knew that I had to prepare myself for it. I dressed my brother. I put him in the stroller and off I went. At the end of a difficult journey, I was in front of the police station, and it was already time for feeding. I took my brother in my lap and walked to the station. I told an officer that I should take the baby to my mother for him to breastfeed. They said, "Your mother is under interrogation, you can't see her." Desperation reverberated in my mind once again. As I was about to walk out of the door in despair, a hand touched my shoulder. This person was a colleague of my father, whom my father extended a helping hand at a time when he was emotionally devastated. He also knew me. He asked what was going on, I told him. "OK come! This is the most natural right of a mother and a baby, no one can prevent this," he said, and took me inside. I went to my mother. I gave her my brother and I started to cry. If my mother was also arrested, this responsibility would be too heavy for me as a child, I was sure of that.

When we were done, we went downstairs to wait. A few hours later, my mother showed up at the door with a group of women like herself in handcuffs. There were dozens of police with them, and I called my mother to find out what was going on. A cop yelled at me, "Shut up! You can't talk." They loaded my mother and all the women with her in a van and took them away. I thought my mom had been arrested because someone had said something about her. My brother was hungry again. I went into a pharmacy and bought the food my mom had told me to buy. I asked for hot water: They said, "There is a tea shop on the upper floor of the bank next door, you can get it from there." I pushed the stroller to the bank, hugged the baby and went upstairs. I asked for hot water. My brother and I were both crying. My tears were preventing me from reading how the food was being made. Bankers gathered around me and asked, "Where is her mother?" I said, "I don't know." They made the food for me. My brother didn't eat. We went outside to avoid further inconvenience at the bank.

A little while later I heard my phone ringing. It was my mother calling. "Are you arrested?" I asked. "Not yet, we just got out of the hospital. We are being taken to the courthouse, they will take our statements and make a decision, take your brother and come there!" she said and hung up the phone. I went to the courthouse. I asked permission to enter again. A police officer helped me and took my brother in. This favor was very important to me. I was waiting for the decision to be made. Hours passed and time was flowing very slowly. If my mother was arrested, I would go to an open high school [which doesn't require attendance]. I decided that in the garden of that courthouse. I searched for information about how to attend open high school on the Internet. I read the releases and made my own plan. Meanwhile, my brother slept, as if he had fallen asleep to do me the greatest favor he could do. This normally uncharacteristic behavior of his relieved me during those hours, or rather gave me free time to pray in fear. My prayers were answered during the evening. My mother was released on probation due to the baby. I looked at the sky and thanked God. I understood what it meant to grow up in a day. The emotions of that short day were so intense that it was worth weeks.

What followed was the process of adapting to our new life. The sadness of my father, who could not witness my brother's growth, was read on his face at every visit. The fact that we lost our financial resources was also a problem in itself. Yet we managed to adapt to that life, with the knowledge that there were dozens of people around us who were experiencing the same things as we were. A miracle happened at the end of two years, and my father was released despite having been sentenced in a court, because his health problems prevented him from being in prison. It was a different kind of festive mood in the house. Shortly after his release, he entered a period of struggle with grueling and long-term health problems as a result of having been in poor prison conditions for two years. It took time to recover and heal the prison wounds, though of course, traces remained. Emotional wounds, in particular, did not heal easily. As someone who has never been there, it is impossible for me to know and understand how much the prison harms one's mental health.

But the effects of the time spent in prison I have seen on my father demonstrated the seriousness and dire nature of the situation. Physical, spiritual, financial... This process had been an incredibly comprehensive destruction in every sense. When my father was released, he said, "being inside is a formidable test and being outside is another formidable test." My father was re-arrested recently after his sentence was upheld after three years outside. We had hoped that his happiness at being able to spend three years with my brother would be a medicine for the sadness of separation from us in the

Stories of Hope

coming years, but it is not.

I still have high hopes that our lives that changed in one day will change once more in one day. I look forward to the beautiful days that await us with hope and excitement.

Assistant Professor Dr. Dogan Yucel

Dogan Yucel was born in 1981 in Turkey's Sivas province. After completing his primary and secondary education in Sivas, he attended Fatih University and graduated from Turkish Language and Literature department in 2004 with his study on "Analysis of Filibeli Hilmi's Journal of Ittihad-i Islam".

He taught Turkish in the cities of Lahore and Karachi in Pakistan between 2004-2011. He completed his postgraduate education at Islamabad National University of Modern Languages Turkish Department in 2013 with his thesis titled "The History of Urdu and Four Main Local Languages in Pakistan, Their Spoken Areas, Sentaxes and Verb Conjugations and a Scan of Turkish Words in Them."

Between 2011 and 2015, he taught Turkish in Sarajevo, Bosnia Herzegovina. He worked as a translator and tourist guide between 2015-2019 and he completed his doctorate education in the meantime with his thesis titled "Phonetic, Morphologic and Thematic Analysis of Turkish-Origin Loanwords in Balkan Languages." He has been teaching Turkish at a secondary school since 2020. He received the title of Assistant Professor in October 2020. He continues to teach general linguistics in International Burch University's master's and doctoral programs. He is fluent in English, Urdu, Bosnian and Serbian, and he can communicate with Punjabi and Arabic for daily conversations. He can read Latin, Cyrillic and Arabic alphabets. His research fields include language and history, interlingual interaction, contact linguistics, language relations, Ottoman cultural history in the Balkans/Middle East, Ottoman poetry, language and culture relations, lexicography and teaching Turkish to foreigners.

He has penned dozens of articles published in scientific journals and written and edited articles for some literary/art journals. He has won various awards on different platforms. He is married and has four wonderful children.

www.ingramcontent.com/pod-product-compliance
Lightning Source LLC
Chambersburg PA
CBHW031625210526
45464CB00004B/1759